Comparing Emerging and Advanced Markets

Comparing Emerging and Advanced Markets

Current Trends and Challenges

Marcus Goncalves and Harry Xia

BEP BUSINESS EXPERT PRESS

First published in 2014 by
Business Expert Press, LLC
222 East 46th Street, New York, NY 10017
www.businessexpertpress.com

ISBN-13: 978-1-63157-015-5 (paperback)
ISBN-13: 978-1-63157-016-2 (e-book)

Business Expert Press Economics Collection

Collection ISSN: 2163-761X (print)
Collection ISSN: 2163-7628 (electronic)

Cover and interior design by Exeter Premedia Services Private Ltd.,
Chennai, India

First edition: 2014

10 9 8 7 6 5 4 3 2 1

Printed in the United States of America.

To my forever-beautiful wife, Carla, and my son Samir, both living here on earth, and to my children Andrea and Joshua, who are now living in Heaven. I also would like to express my gratitude for my mother-in-law, Maria Duenas, for her gentle and loving care for me, especially during the intense research times where I'd forget to eat; she was always there with a smoothie to keep me going.

To God be the glory!

Marcus Goncalves
Summer 2014

Abstract

This book is a part of a series, which recognizes that there is intense competition among emerging markets and against advanced economies to capture their share of the global economy. The series addresses questions that are germane to accomplishing this goal. Most important to this end is the study and practice of international business and foreign trade. Undertaking such a study raises many questions, which the series will attempt to answer. What competitive advantages do these emerging economies enjoy in comparison to advanced economies, such as the G7, and what are the origins of those advantages? Why are emerging markets becoming the powerhouse of world economy growth and the firms doing business there internationalizing so aggressively? And, why in the past decade has the pace of internationalization accelerated so rapidly and what are the challenges and possible solutions? This volume is devoted to a comparison of advanced economies and emerging ones, the advantages and disadvantages of each, and what globalization means in each type of environment.

Keywords

advanced economies, emerging markets, frontier markets, global economy, global trade

Contents

Acknowledgments

There were many people who helped us during the process of writing this book. It would be impossible to keep track of them all. Therefore, to all that we have forgotten to list, please don't hold it against us!

We would like to thank Dr. Patrick Barron, professor at the Graduate School of Banking at the University of Wisconsin, Madison, and of Austrian economics at the University of Iowa, in Iowa City for his contributions on the issue of currency wars in Chapter 5. Many thanks also to ambassador M. K. Bhadrakumar, former diplomat in the Indian Foreign Service with assignments in the Soviet Union, South Korea, Sri Lanka, Germany, Afghanistan, Pakistan, Uzbekistan, Kuwait, and Turkey for his valuable insights and contributions to foreign policy issues in the MENA region.

CHAPTER 1

The Influence of the G-7 Advanced Economies and G-20 Group

Overview

When we think of the G-20 countries, whose summit took place in St. Petersburg, Russia, on September 5th through the 6th, 2013, we should think about the group of 20 finance ministers and central bankers from the 20 major economies around the world. In essence, the G-20 is comprised of 19 countries plus the European Union (EU), represented by the president of the European Council and by the European Central Bank (ECB). We begin this book discussing the importance and influence of the G-20, not only does this group comprise some of the most advancing economies in the world, collectively these 20 economies account for approximately 80 percent of the gross world product (GWP); 80 percent of the world's trade, which includes EUs intra-trade; and about two-thirds of the world's population.[*] These proportions are not expected to change radically for many decades to come.

The G-20, proposed by the former Canadian Prime Minister Paul Martin,[1] acts as a forum for cooperation and consultation on matters pertaining to the international financial system. Since its inception in September of 1999, the group has been studying, reviewing, and promoting high-level discussions of policy issues concerning the promotion of international financial stability. The group has replaced the G-8 group as the main economic council of wealthy nations.[2] Although not popular with many political activists and intellectuals, the group exercises major influence on economic and financial policies around the world.

---

[*] G-20 membership from the official G-20 website at www.g20.org

G20 Countries	
Argentina	Japan
Australia	Mexico
Brazil	Russia
Canada	Saudia Arabia
China	South Africa
France	South Korea
Germany	Turkey
India	United Kingdom
Indonesia	United States
Italy	European Union

Figure 1.1 G-20 country list

The G-20 Summit was created as a response both to the financial crisis of 2007 to 2010 and to a growing recognition that key emerging countries (and markets) were not adequately included in the core of global economic discussion and governance. The G-20 country members are listed in Figure 1.1.

It is important to note that the G-20 members do not necessarily reflect the 20 largest economies of the world in any given year. According to the group, as defined in its FAQs, there are "no formal criteria for G-20 membership, and the composition of the group has remained unchanged since it was established. In view of the objectives of the G-20, it was considered important that countries and regions of systemic significance of the international financial system be included. Aspects such as geographical balance and population representation also played a major part."[3] All 19-member nations, however, are among the top 30 economies as measured in gross domestic product (GDP) at nominal prices according to a list published by the International Monetary Fund (IMF)[4] in April 2013. That being said, the G-20 list does not include some of the top 30 economies in the world as ranked by the World Bank[5] and depicted in Figure 1.2, such as Switzerland (19th), Thailand (30th), Norway (24th) and Taiwan (29th), despite the fact that economies rank higher than some of the member countries in the G-20. In the EU, the largest economies

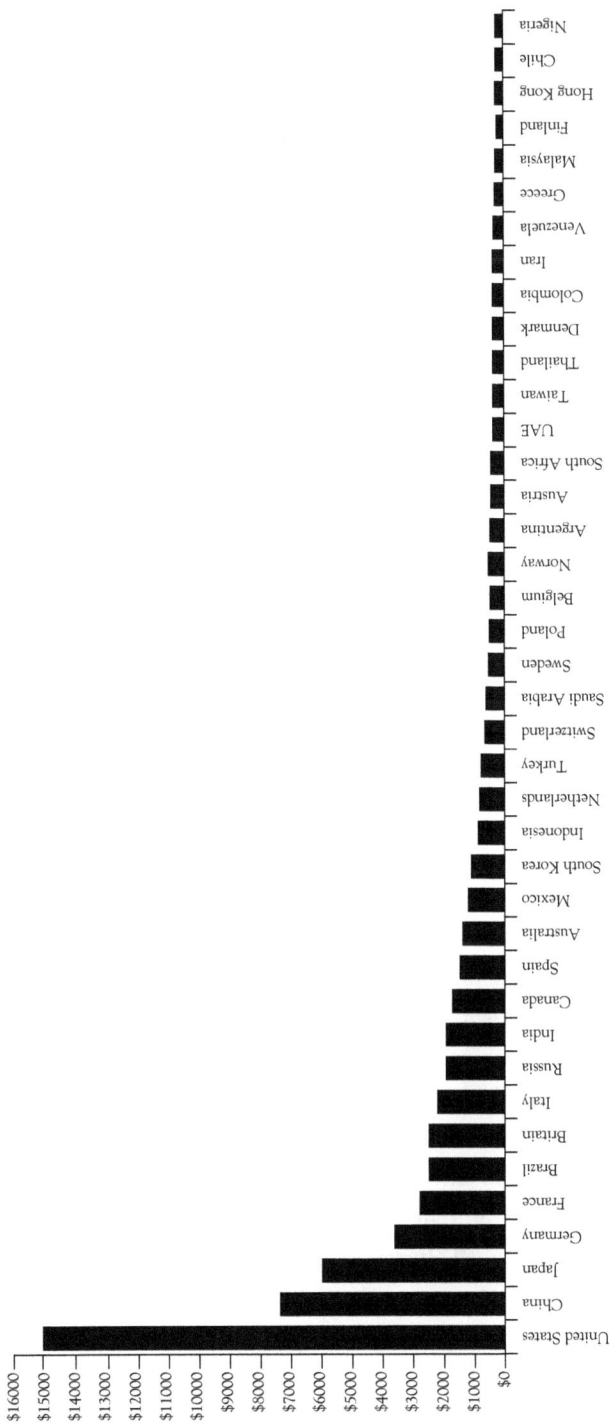

Figure 1.2 World Bank top 40 countries by GDP

are Spain (13th), the Netherlands (18th), Sweden (22nd), Poland (24th), Belgium (25th) and Austria (28th). These economies are ranked as part of the EU though, and not independently.

Asian economies, such as China (2nd) and India (10th), are expected to play an important role in global economic governance, according to the Asian Development Bank (ADB), as the rise of emerging market economies are heralding a new world order. The G-20 would likely become the global economic steering committee. Furthermore, not only have Asian countries been leading the global recovery following the *great recession*, but key indicators also suggest the region will have a greater presence on the global stage, especially considering the latest advances in GDP for countries such as Thailand and the Philippines. These trends are shaping the G-20 agenda for balanced and sustainable growth through strengthening intraregional trade and stimulating domestic demand.[6]

The G-8 and G-20 Group Influence in the Global Economy

The G-8 and G-20 are coalitions of nations, who address significant international issues. The predecessor of both coalitions was the G-7, a group of seven nations, which banded together in 1975 to oppose the 1973 oil embargo by various Arab nations. The Arabs put the embargo into place as a protest against the intervention of the United States and the United Kingdom during the Yom Kippur War. The Arab nations waged war with Israel, but were unsuccessful because the United States and United Kingdom provided Israel with weapons and military might.

The U.S.S.R., which was by then on the verge of breaking up, supplied the Arab nations with weapons, and because of this move was not included in the G-7. The G-7 was known formally as the Group of Seven Industrialized Nations. It was composed of Britain, United States, France, Canada, Japan, Italy, and Germany. The G-7 was renamed as the G-8 during 1997, when Russia was added to the original seven-country lineup. Ever since its inception, the G-7 and G-8 asserted several political and economic policies, which affected other countries.

The G-7 and G-8 became known in the international scene as the major policy-makers, which could enforce or disrupt political and economic stability. The latest installment of the G-8 is called the G-20, a greater coalition formed in 1999 that included the nations of Brazil, China, Saudi Arabia, Republic of Korea, France, Australia, China, Canada, Germany, Indonesia, Argentina, Turkey, India, Russia, South Africa, Mexico, Japan, United Kingdom, United States, and the European Union.

While the G-20 is supposed to acknowledge all members as equals, it cannot be denied that the countries, which were included in its G-8 predecessor, have an advantage over other countries in terms of political and economic policy-making. So far, the G-20 goals for 2014 are to focus on growth and resilience.

G-20 country growth strategies contain a mix of macroeconomic and structural reforms at the domestic level that suit each country's circumstances in areas with the greatest potential to lift global growth:

- **Increasing quality investment in infrastructure.** This will create jobs and boost economic growth and development. The G-20 is focusing on finding ways to boost private sector involvement in infrastructure development.
- **Reducing barriers to trade.** Many products are not made solely in one country and sold somewhere else, but cross national borders many times as they are created. Domestic measures to cut the cost of doing business and enhance countries' ability to participate in global value chains can facilitate increased trade activity, fueling economic growth.
- **Promoting competition.** Reforms to promote competition help economies become more productive and innovative, and can bring prices closer to production costs, benefiting consumers and encouraging business to become more efficient.
- **Lifting employment and participation.** More and better jobs mean a more productive economy, leading to improved livelihoods and increased economic growth.

Strengthening development is an important part of achieving strong, sustainable and balanced growth, and ensuring a more robust and resilient economy for everyone. According to the International Monetary Fund, emerging markets and developing economies contribute more than two thirds of global growth.

For 2014, G-20 members are building the resilience of the global economy by:

- delivering on the G-20's core financial regulation reforms;
- modernizing the international tax system to keep pace with the changing ways people and companies do business;
- reforming global institutions to ensure countries that are reshaping the global economy have a greater voice and keep the institutions relevant;
- strengthening energy market resilience, improving the operation of global energy markets for greater efficiency, and transparency;
- fighting corruption.

Prior to the G-20 enjoying the influence it has today in global economic policy-making, the G-8 group was the leading global economic policy forum. Figure 1.3 illustrates the breakdown of the G-8 countries by population. The U.S. population is about 300 million people, which is roughly a third of the population of all of the G-8 countries

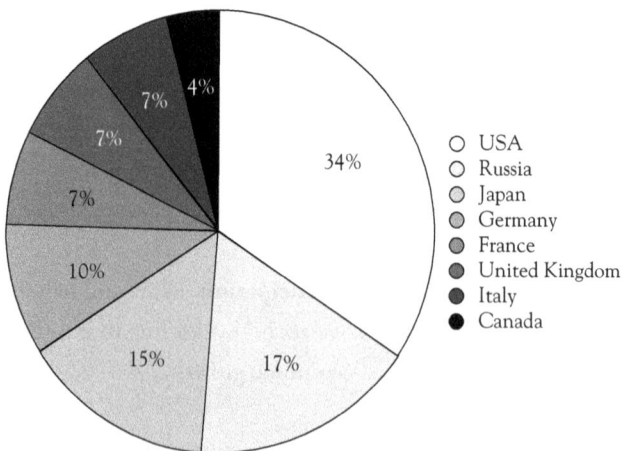

Figure 1.3 List of G-8 countries by power of influence

Source: CIA World Factbook.

combined—equal to Japan and Russia combined, and to Germany, France, Italy, Canada, and the United Kingdom combined.

As the world economy continues to be increasingly integrated, the need for a global hub, a forum where the world economy issues and challenges could converge, is a major necessity. In the absence of a complete overhaul of the United Nations (UN) and international financial institutions, such as the IMF and the World Bank, the G-20 is the only viable venue to mitigate the interests of these leading nations. Since this group has overshadowed the G-8, it has become a major forum for global decision making, central to designing a pathway out of the worst global financial crisis in almost a century. It did so by effectively coordinating the many individual policies adopted by its members and thus establishing its importance in terms of crisis management and coordination during an emergency.

The G-20 has failed, thus far, to live up to expectations as a viable alternative to the G-8, although it continues to be at the heart of global power shifts, particularly to emerging markets. Efforts to reform the international financial system have produced limited results. It has struggled to deliver on its 2010 summit promises on fiscal consolidation and banking capital, while the world watches the global finance lobbyists repeatedly demonstrate their ability to thwart every G-20's attempts to regulate financial flows, despite the volatility associated with the movement of large amounts of short-term funds. Hence, its goals for 2014 were met with skepticism.

Larger economies, such as Germany and Spain, have been concerned with the lack of effective regulation of financial flows. Emerging markets such as the BRIC (Brazil, Russia, India, and China) countries and the CIVETS (Colombia, Indonesia, Vietnam, Egypt, Turkey, and South Africa*) countries are scrambling to deflect the exportation of inflation from these advanced G-8 economies into their domestic economies. Countries such as Iceland, the UK, and Ireland, whose banking systems had to undergo painful recapitalization, nationalization, and restructuring to return to profitability after the financial crisis broke, also share these concerns.

---

* It is important to note that although South Africa is grouped with the CIVETS bloc, it also has been aggregated to the BRIC bloc, where it is more likely to belong.

In the words of Ian Bremmer*, in his 2013 book titled *Every Nation for Itself: Winners and Losers in a G-Zero World*,[7] when reflecting on the then newly created G-20 group, "I found myself imagining an enormous poker table where each player guards his stack of chips, watches the nineteen others, and waits for an opportunity to play the hand he has been dealt. This is not a global order, but every nation for itself. *And if the G-7 no longer matters and the G-20 doesn't work, then what is this world we now live in?*"[†]

According to Bremmer, we now are living in a time where the world has no global leadership since, he argues, the United States can no longer provide such leadership to the world due to its "endless partisan combat and mounting federal debt."[‡] He also argues that Europe can't provide any leadership either as debt crisis is crippling confidence in the region, its institutions, and its future. In his view the same goes for Japan, which is still recovering from a devastating earthquake, tsunami, and nuclear meltdown, in addition to the more than two decades of political and economic malaise. Institutions like the UN Security Council, the IMF, and the World Bank are unlikely to provide real leadership because they no longer reflect the world's true balance of political and economic power. The fact is, a generation ago the G-7 were the world's powerhouses, the group of free-market democracies that powered the global economy. Today, they struggle just to find their footing.

In Bremmer's view, "The G-Zero phenomenon and resulting lack of global leadership have only intensified—and analysts from conservative political scientist Francis Fukuyama to liberal Nobel Prize winning economist Joseph Stiglitz have since written of the G-Zero as a fact of international life."[§] "The G-Zero," Bremmer continues, "won't last forever, but over the next decade and perhaps longer, a world without leaders will undermine our ability to keep the peace, to expand opportunity, to reverse the impact of climate change, and to feed growing populations. The effects will be felt in every nation of the word—and even in cyberspace."[¶]

---

* Bremmer is the president of the Eurasia Group, the world's leading global political risk research and consulting firm.

† Emphasis is ours.

‡ Ibidem, pg 3.

§ Ibidem, pg VIII.

¶ Ibidem, pg 5.

Coping With Shifting Power Dynamics in a Multipolar World

In the past decade, the emerging markets have been growing at a much faster pace than the advanced economies. Consequently, participation in the global gross domestic product (GDP), global trade, and foreign direct investment (FDI), particularly in the global financial markets, has significantly increased as well. Such trends, according to a study conducted by the Banco de Espana's analysts Orgaz, Molina, and Carrasco,[8] are expected to continue for the next few years. The global economic crises actually has fostered relevant changes to the governance of the global economy, particularly with the substitution of the G-8 with the G-20 group as a leading international forum in the development of global economic policies.

The G-20's failure to effectively regulate global financial flows has led to efforts to reclaim national sovereignty through so-called host or home-country financial regulations, as national legislative bodies seek control over financial flows. The impetus for both can be found in the changing global order as it moves toward greater global balance.

For many decades various other groups, such as the G-7; the Non-aligned Movement; India, Brazil, South Africa (IBSA); and the BRICS, to name the main ones, have been applying some informal pressure, largely reflecting the continued north-south or advanced versus emerging markets, divide into global geopolitics and wealth. Although financial analysts and policy makers in the advanced economies tend to view the G-20 as a venue to build and extend the outreach of global consensus on their policies, such expectations have been changing due to the establishment of a loose coalition with a distinctly contrarian view on many global issues. This is particularly true in regard to the role of the state in development and on finance.

This loose coalition, which has become more prominent since the global financial crises of 2008, is spearheaded by the BRICS (the "S" is for South Africa), led by China. While Chapter seven provides a more in-depth discussion on the role of the BRICS in this process, for now it is important to note how the BRICS countries are able to apply pressure on the G-20 group, particularly to advanced economies.

The BRICS cohort within the G-20 has a combined GDP three times smaller than that of the G-7. Nonetheless, the gap between the two decreases every year and is expected to disappear within the next two decades, if not sooner. Even more importantly, most of the economic growth within the G-20 is coming from the BRICS (and other emerging and so called "frontier" markets) rather than from the advanced economies (the G-7). Hence, while there are many other geopolitical dynamics playing out within the G-20, we believe the most important play at the moment and in the next two decades is a battle for strategic positioning by the advanced economies versus the emerging markets, who are led by the BRICS. Even more important is to watch as the BRICS jockey for support from other G-20 members such as Indonesia, Mexico, Saudi Arabia, and Turkey. While some allegiances may appear obvious, economic and political benefits often pull in opposite directions, leaving policy makers with difficult choices to make.

In order for the G-20 countries to continue to build on their collective success in the management of the global financial crisis, it is imperative for them to place more emphasis on global trade and financial reform. These elements are at the core of global trade and economic governance. Unfortunately, advanced economies, particularly in North America and Europe, are heading in a different direction than the emerging ones, particularly the BRICS, as a result of the shifting power dynamics in an increasingly multipolar world. In the past decade China prominently has exercised this shift.

Such shifting of power dynamics, or the fight to control it, is perhaps most evident in the efforts toward exclusive trade agreements in the Atlantic and Pacific oceans, such as the Transatlantic Trade and Investment Partnership (TTIP), where discussions began in July of 2013 between the United States and Europe. Similarly, the Trans-Pacific Partnership (TPP) also discussed collaborating with eleven other countries, including Japan.

TTIP's purpose is to remove the regulatory differences between the United States and European nations, but purposely or not, the agreement enables a remarkable ability for big business to sue governments, which may be trying to defend their citizens. It would allow a secretive panel of corporate lawyers to overrule the will of government and destroy legal protections. It is a concern to government institutions, especially since defenders of sovereignty are not saying much.

For example, during its financial crisis, and in response to public anger over rocketing charges, Argentina imposed a freeze on people's energy and water bills. In response, the international utility companies, whose vast bills had prompted the government to act, sued the federal government. For this and other such crimes, it has been forced to pay out over a billion dollars in compensation. Another example is El Salvador, were local communities managed at great cost (three campaigners were murdered) to persuade the government to refuse permission for a vast gold mine, which threatened to contaminate their water supplies. The Canadian company, which sought to dig the mine, is now suing El Salvador for $315 million–for the loss of its anticipated future profits.[9]

As a trade and investment agreement, TTIP's main objective is to drive growth and create jobs by removing trade barriers in a wide range of economic sectors, making it easier to buy and sell goods and services between the EU and the United States. A research study conducted by the Centre for Economic Policy Research, in London-UK, titled *Reducing Trans-Atlantic Barriers to Trade and Investment: An Economic Assessment,*[10] suggests that TTIP could boost the EU's economy by €120 billion euros ($197 billion), while also boosting the U.S. economy by €90 billion euros ($147.75 billion) and the rest of the world by €100 billion euros ($164.16 billion).

The success of TTIP and TPP could undermine the future viability of the World Trade Organization (WTO) as a global trade forum, such as the Doha Round. Although not isolated, China is party to neither group. The unspoken concern is that the two agreements are aimed at ensuring continued Western control of the global economy by building a strong relationship between the euro and the dollar while constraining and containing a growing and increasingly assertive China.

Since 2010, the United States has been negotiating a secret trade deal, that is, the TPP. If approved by Congress, this pact between the United States and 11 or 12 of America's Pacific Rim trade-partners would govern 40 percent of U.S. imports and exports. So far, the negotiations have been conducted under tight security; for good reason, as there are big problems with the TPP. It suffers from a severe lack of transparency, particularly as

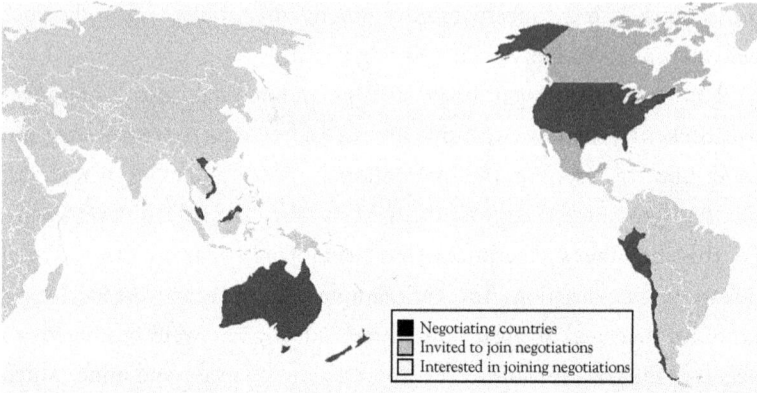

Figure 1.4 The Trans-Pacific Partnership eleven member countries

U.S. negotiators push for the adoption of copyright measures far more constraining than currently required by international treaties, including the polemic Anti-Counterfeiting Trade Agreement (ACTA). The treaty, while also attempting to rewrite global rules on intellectual property enforcement is nonetheless a free trade agreement, which (as of fall 2013) is being negotiated by twelve countries. As depicted in Figure 1.4, these countries include the United States, Japan, Australia, Peru, Malaysia, Vietnam, New Zealand, Chile, Singapore, Canada, Mexico, and Brunei Darussalam.

According to Bob Burnett,[11] a retired Silicon Valley executive, there are major problems with TPP as it stands today:

1. U.S. trade negotiators want TPP to get special, "fast-track" treatment from Congress. While Congress has the legal duty to oversee trade agreements, in the past it has given up some of that responsibility to the president. Under a fast-track arrangement, trade agreements such as TPP, would simply get an up or down vote without Congress delving into the details. The previous fast-track authorization lapsed in 2007 and now the Obama administration wants Congress to restore it so that TPP will be approved with a minimum of fuss.

   Interestingly, most Republicans are willing to give fast-track trade authority to President Obama even though they don't trust him on other issues, primarily because powerful transnational corporations want the Trans-Pacific Partnership to be approved. The U.S. Chamber of Commerce stated, "Completing the TPP would pay huge dividends for the United States. The agreement would significantly improve U.S. companies' access to the Asia-Pacific region, which is projected to import nearly $10 trillion worth of goods in 2020."*

2. **TPP doesn't include China.** The TPP partners are Australia, Brunei, Chile, Japan, Malaysia, Mexico, New Zealand, Canada, Peru, Singapore, Vietnam, and potentially Korea. But the Economic Policy Institute reported that since 2001, "the U.S. has lost 2.7 million jobs… due to growing trade deficits with China."[12] The American Manufacturing website noted that approximately 40 percent of the U.S. trade deficit is due to China.

3. **Free-trade agreements, such as TPP, haven't protected U.S. jobs.** Public Citizen reported that since 1994, "the [free-trade agreement] deficit surge implies the loss of nearly one million American jobs."[13] Public Citizen said, "wherever there were free-trade agreements, U.S. trade deficits increased, and in the countries not covered by free-trade agreements, our deficits decreased."

4. **If TPP were to be approved, most of the benefit would go to corporations and the rich.** Public Citizen reported, "The TPP would mean wage losses for all but the richest 10 percent of U.S. workers."†

Overall, the TPP will affect countries beyond the 11 that are currently involved in negotiations. Like ACTA, the TPP Agreement is a multilateral agreement that will be used to create new heightened global intellectual property (IP) enforcement norms. Countries that are not privy to the negotiation will likely be asked to accede to the TPP as a condition of bilateral trade agreements with the United States and other TPP members, or evaluated against the TPP's copyright enforcement standards in the annual Special 301 process administered by the U.S. Trade Rep.

The Impact of Indebtedness of the Advanced Economies on Emerging Markets

In September 2013, Canadian Prime Minister Stephen Harper vehemently urged G-20 leaders not to lose sight of the vital importance of

---

* https://www.uschamber.com/issue-brief/trans-pacific-partnership
† Ibidem.

reining in debt across the group. This comes after several years of deficit-fueled stimulus spending and sticking to a common refrain in the face
of weak recoveries among member countries, including Canada. Specifically referring to the risk of accumulating public debt points, Mr. Harper
also acknowledged that recoveries from the financial crisis that started five
years ago have been disappointing because many of the advanced economies continue to grapple with high unemployment, weak growth, and
rising income inequality.

Since the economic crisis of 2008, the United States and its financial
analysts and politicians have been very vocal with ideas of *fiscal cliffs*, debt
ceiling, and defaults. To some extent, the situation is not much different
among the EU block. Debt to GDP ratios and deficit figures have been
touted as omens of financial failure, and public debt has been heralded
as the harbinger of an apocalypse. The truth of the matter is that many
countries around the world, especially in the emerging markets during
the 70s and 80s, had experienced large amounts of debt, often in excess of
100 percent of GDP, as advanced economies are experiencing right now.
Nonetheless, what is different this time is that while emerging markets
had most of their debt in external markets and denominated in foreign
currencies, they also had differing structures and institutions than the
advanced economies.

The last quarter of the (19th) century was a period of large accumulation
of debt due to widespread infrastructure building in advanced economies
around the globe, mainly due to the new innovations at the time, such
as the railroads. As these economies expanded and continued to invest in
infrastructure, much debt was created. This was true during World War I
(WWI) which reflected the military spending undertaken during the war-
time period, and immediately after that during the reconstruction period.
Another period of large debt was amassed during and post—World War
II (WWII). In this case, some of these debt levels started to build a bit earlier, as a result of the great recession, but most were the result of WWII.
Finally, we have the period where most governments and policymakers of
advanced economies struggled to move from the old economic systems
to the current one. During these four different periods, most advanced
economies experienced 100 percent or more debt to GDP ratios at least
one or more times. The dynamics of debt to GDP ratios are in fact very

diverse; their effects are widely varied and based on a variety of factors. Take for example the case of the UK in 1918, the United States in 1946, Belgium in 1983, Italy in 1992, Canada in 1995, and Japan in 1997. All of these countries went through a process of indebtedness, each with a full range of outcomes.

In the case of England, policymakers tried to return to the gold standard at pre-WWI levels to restore trade, prosperity, and prestige, and to pay off as much debt, as quickly as possible to preserve the image of British good credit. They sought to achieve these goals through policies that included thrift saving. Their efforts did not have the intended effects. The dual pursuit of going back to a strengthened currency from a devalued one and, along with, the pursuit of fiscal austerity seemed to be a deciding factor in the failure. Trying to go back to the gold standard that had not depreciated made British exports less attractive than those of surrounding countries who had not chosen this path. Consequently, exports were low. To combat this, British banks kept interest rates high. Those high interest rates meant that the debt the country was trying to pay off increased in value and the country's slow growth and austerity did not give them the economic power to pay off the debts as they wanted. In trying to maintain integrity and the image of "old faithful Britain," the policymakers ruined their chances for swift recovery.

In the United States, policymakers chose not to control inflation, and kept a floor on government bonds. Over time, these ideas changed and bond protection measures were lifted. In turn, the government's ability to intervene in inflation situations changed. The United States experienced rapid growth during this time, partially due to high levels of monetary inflation, but that inflation, even though it would "burst" at the start of the Korean War, allowed the United States to pay off much of its debt. This, coupled with the floor on U.S. bonds, created a favorable post high debt level scenario.

Japan's initial response to its debt situation was the cutting of inflation rates and the introduction of fiscal stimulus programs. This response did not have the intended effect, as currency appreciated. The underlying issues that had helped to cause the high debt to GDP ratios were still present, and would be until 2001, when the government committed to boosting the country's economy through policy and structure changes. Japan still has a very high debt to GDP ratio, but the weaknesses in the banking sector have been fixed, and the country seems to be on a path to recovery.

Italy's attempts at fiscal reform included changes to many social programs, including large cuts to pension spending. The reforms, though, were not implemented quickly enough and did not address enough of the demographic issues to make a large impact. It wasn't until later that further fiscal consolidation was achieved. It is important to note that Italy's GDP growth did not help reduce debt during this period, and thus remained very weak.

Belgium used similar kinds of fiscal consolidation plans to those of Italy, but those plans were more widespread and implemented at a more rapid pace. The relative success of these initial fiscal consolidations helped to further growth and reduction of the debt to GDP ratio. These plans also fueled another round of successful consolidation when the country needed it to enter the EU.

Canada's initial reaction included fiscal changes such as tax hikes and spending cuts; a plan of austerity. The plan failed and deepened the country's debt. The second wave of fiscal consolidation was aimed at fixing some of the structural imbalances that had caused the debt levels in the first place. It worked, helped along by the strengthening of economic conditions in surrounding countries, mainly the United States. The Canadian example shows that the external conditions are just as important for success as the policies or missions taken on within the country experiencing high debt ratios.

From all of these examples, we have an idea of the impact that advanced economies have on each other as well as on emerging markets. In an intertwined global economy, imbalances in one country's economy impact virtually every other country in the world. The extent of the impacts and mitigation will always vary depending on internal and external market conditions, as well as policy development. Similarly solutions, like the U.S. inflation adjustments, may not work today or in another country. For instance, if we take the global financial crises that started in 2008, allowing inflation levels to rise could pose risks to the financial institutions, and could lead to a globally less—integrated financial system.

The most pertinent example would appear to be the kind of fiscal policies used in Canada, Belgium, and Italy. All three countries attempted to achieve low inflation, but their other policy reforms varied in success. More permanent fiscal changes tend to create more prominent and lasting reductions to debt levels. Even then, a country must be exposed to an increase in external demands if the country's recovery is going to mirror the successful cases cited earlier. Consolidation needs to be implemented alongside measures to support growth and changes that address structural issues. The final factor to note is that even with a successful plan, the effects of the plan take time. Debt level reductions will not be quick in today's global and interwoven economies.

The Crisis Isn't Over Yet

Advanced economies, specifically in the EU and the United States are still dealing with the global financial crises that started in 2008. Despite the positive rhetoric of policy makers and governments on both sides of the Atlantic, Harvard economist Carmen Reinhart feels that the crisis is not yet over. She alleges that both the U.S. Federal Reserve and the European Central Bank (ECB) are keeping interest rates low to help governments out of their debt crises. In the past and as shown in the historial examples, central banks are bending over backwards to help governments of advanced economies to finance their deficits.

As was mentioned earlier in this chapter, after WWII all countries that had a big debt overhang relied on financial repression to avoid an explicit default, and governments imposed interest rate ceilings for government bonds. Liberal capital-market regulations and international capital mobility at the time reached their peak prior to WWI under the gold standard. But, the Great Depression, followed by WWII, put the final nails in the coffin of laissez-faire banking.* It was in this environment that the Bretton Woods arrangement of fixed exchange rates and tightly controlled domestic and international capital markets was conceived. The result was a combination of very low interest rates and inflationary spurts of varying degrees across the advanced economies. The obvious results were real interest rates–whether on treasury bills, central bank discount

---

* An economic theory from the 18th century that is strongly opposed to any government intervention in business affairs

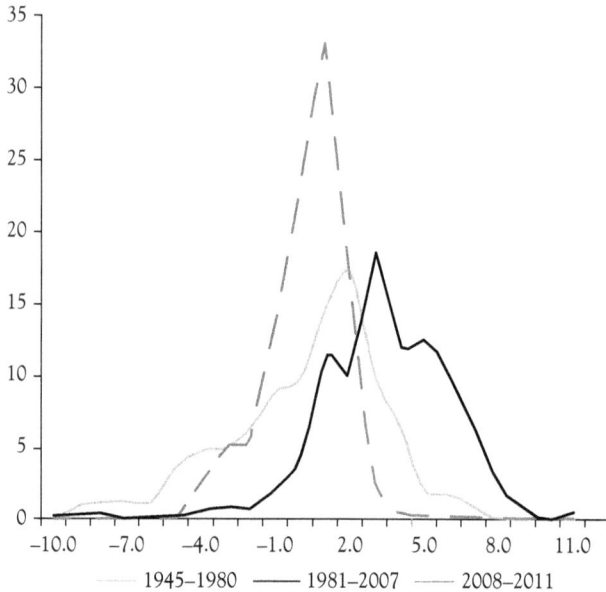

Figure 1.5 Real interest rates frequency distributions: advanced economies, 1945–2011

rates, deposits or loans–that were markedly negative during 1945 to 46. For the next 35 years, real interest rates in both advanced and emerging economies would remain consistently lower than during the eras of free capital mobility, including before and after the financial repression era. Ostensibly, real interest rates were, on average, negative. The frequency distributions of real rates for the period of financial repression (1945 to 1980) and the years following financial liberalization highlight the universality of lower real interest rates prior to the 1980s and the high incidence of negative real interest rates in the advanced economies (Figure 1.5). Reinhart and Sbrancia[14] (2011) demonstrate a comparable pattern for the emerging markets.

Nowadays, however, monetary policy is doing the job, but unlike many policy makers would like us to believe these economies are seldom able to break out of debt. Money to pay for these debts must come from somewhere. Reinhart* (2011) believes those advanced economies in debt today must adopt a combination of austerity to restrain the trend

---

* Ibidem.

of adding to the stack of debt and higher inflation. This is effectively a subtle form of taxation and consequently will cause a depreciation of the currency and erode people's savings.

We do not advocate for or against current central bank policies in these economies; this is not premise of this book. Advanced economies, however, *do* need to deal with their debt as these high debt levels prevent growth and freeze the financial system and the credit process. As long as emerging markets continue to depend heavily on the exports of these advanced economies, they too will be negatively impacted. We believe, however, that the debt of the United States and the EU, in particular, affects the global economy significantly. The current central bank policies are not effective; as money is being transferred from responsible savers to borrowers via negative interest rates.

In essence, when the inflation rate is higher than the interest rates paid on the markets, the debts shrink as if by magic. As dubbed by Ronald McKinnon[15] (1973), the term *financial repression* describes various policies that allow governments to *capture* and *under-pay* domestic savers. Such policies include forced lending to governments by pension funds and other domestic financial institutions, interest-rate caps, capital controls, and many more. Typically, governments use a mixture of these policies to bring down debt levels, but inflation and financial repression usually only work for domestically held debt. The eurozone is a special hybrid case. The financial repression implemented by advanced economies is designed to avoid an explicit default on the debt. Unfortunately, this is not only ineffective in the long run but also unjust to responsible taxpayers. Eventually public revolts may develop, such as the ones already witnessed in Greece and Spain. Governments could write off part of the debt, but evidently no politician would be willing to spearhead such write-offs. After all, most citizens do not realize their savings are being eroded and that there is a major transfer of wealth taking place. Undeniably, advanced economies around the world have a problem with debt. In the past, several tactics, including financial repression, have dealt with such problems, and now it seems, debt is resurging again in the wake of the global and eurozone crises.

Financial repression, coupled with a steady dose of inflation, cuts debt burdens from two directions. First the introduction of low nominal interest rates reduces debt-servicing costs. Secondly, negative real interest rates erode the debt-to-GDP ratio. In other words, this is a tax on savers. Financial repression also has some noteworthy political-economic properties. Unlike other taxes, the "repression" tax rate is determined by financial regulations and inflation performance, which are obscure to the highly politicized realm of fiscal measures. Given that deficit reduction usually involves highly unpopular expenditure reductions and tax increases of one form or another, the relatively *stealthier* financial repression tax may be a more politically palatable alternative for authorities faced with the need to reduce outstanding debts. In such an environment, inflation, by historic standards, does not need to be very high or take market participants entirely by surprise.

Unlike the United States, which is resorting to financial repression, Europe is focusing more on austerity measures; despite the fact inflation is still at a low level. Notwithstanding, debt restructuring, inflation, and financial repression, are not a substitute for austerity. All these measures reduce a country's existing stock of debt, and as argued by Reinhart,[16] policy makers need a combination of both to bring down debt to a sustainable level. Although the United States is highly indebted, an advantage it has against all other advanced economies is that foreign central banks are the ones holding most of its debts. The Bank of China and the Bank of Brazil, two leading BRICS emerging economies, are not likely to be repaid. It does not mean the United States will default. We don't know that, no one does. It actually doesn't have to explicitly default since if you have negative real interest rates, the effect on the creditors is the same, a transfer from China and Brazil, as well as other creditors to the United States.

The real risk here for the United States, EU, and other advanced economies is that creditors may decide not to play along anymore, which would cause interest rates on American government bonds to climb. This act would be similar to the major debt crises of Greece and Iceland and what was happening in Spain until the ECB intervened. We believe the U.S. Federal Reserve Bank, and likely the ECB, is prepared to continue buying record levels of debt for as long as it takes to jump-start the economy. To counter the debasement of the dollar, China's central bank is likely continue to buy U.S. treasury bonds in a constant attempt to stop the export of inflation from the United States into its economy and by preventing the renminbi from appreciating. In an attempt to save their economies from indebtedness, advanced economies are raging what Jim Rickards calls a *currency war* against the emerging markets and the rest of the world.

We believe the combination of high public and private debts in the advanced economies and the perceived dangers of currency misalignments and overvaluation in emerging markets facing surges of capital inflows, are causing pressures toward currency intervention and capital controls, interacting to produce a home-bias in finance, and a resurgence of financial repression. At present, we find that emerging markets, especially the BRICS, are being forced to adopt similar policies as the advanced economies—hence the *currency wars*—but not as a financial repression, but more in the context of *macroprudential* regulations.

Advanced economies are developing financial regulatory measures to keep international capital out of emerging economies, and in advanced economies. Such economic controls are intended to counter loose monetary policy in the advanced economies and discourage the so-called *hot money**, while regulatory changes in advanced economies are meant to create a captive audience for domestic debt. This offers advanced and emerging market economies common ground on tighter restrictions on international financial flows, which borderlines protectionism policies. More broadly, the world is witnessing a return to a more tightly regulated domestic financial environment, that is, financial repression.

We believe advanced economies are imposing a major strain on global financial markets, in particular emerging economies, by exporting inflation to those countries. Because governments are incapable of reducing their debts, central banks are pressured to get involved in an attempt to resolve the crisis. Reinhart argues that such a policy does not come cheap, and those responsible citizens and everyday savers will be the ones feeling the consequences of such policies the most. While no central bank will admit it is purposely keeping interest rates low to help governments out of their debt crises, banks are doing whatever they can to help these economies finance their deficits.

---

* Capital that is frequently transferred between financial institutions in an attempt to maximize interest or capital gain.

The major danger of such a central bank policy, which can be at first very detrimental to emerging markets that are still largely dependent on consumer demands from advanced economies, is that it can lead to high inflation. As inflation rises among advanced economies, it is also exported to emerging market's economies. In other words, as the U.S. dollar and the euro debases and loses buying power, emerging markets experience an artificial strengthening of their currency, courtesy of the U.S. Federal Reserve and the ECB. In turn, this causes the prices of their goods and services to also increase and hurts exports in the process.

Figure 1.5, shown earlier, strikingly shows that real export interest rates (shown for treasury bills) for the advanced economies have, once again, turned increasingly negative since the outbreak of the crisis in 2008. Real rates have been negative for about one half of the observations, and below one percent for about 82 percent of the observations. This turn to lower real interest rates has materialized despite the fact that several sovereigns have been teetering on the verge of default or restructuring. Indeed, in recent months negative yields in most advanced economies, the G-7 countries, have moved much further outside the yield curve, as depicted in Figure 1.6.

No doubt, a critical factor explaining the high incidence of negative real interest rates in the wake of the crisis is the aggressive expansive stance

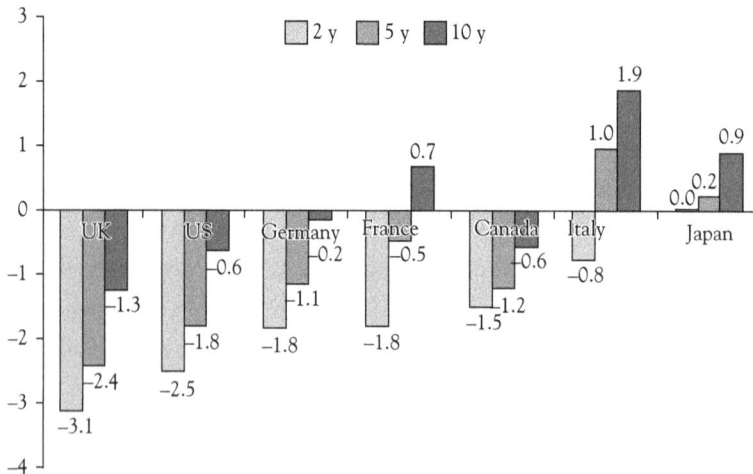

Figure 1.6 G-7 real government bond yields, February 2012

of monetary policy, particularly the official central bank interventions in many advanced and emerging economies during this period.

At the time of this writing in the fall of 2013, the levels of public debt in many advanced economies is at their highest levels, with some economies facing the prospect of debt restructuring. Moreover, public and private external debts, which we should not ignore, are typically a volatile source of funding, are at historic highs. The persistent levels of unemployment in many advanced economies also are still high. These negative trends offer further motivation for central banks and policy makers to keep interest rates low, posing a renewed taste for financial repression. Hence, we believe the final crisis isn't over yet. The impact that advanced economies are imposing on emerging markets, and its own economies, is only the tip of a very large iceberg.

CHAPTER 2

The Counter-Influence of Emerging Markets Across the Globe

Overview

The emerging markets have been the source of global economic growth for quite some time now, with far-reaching effects to the rest of the world, in particular to advanced economies. It is not news that emerging markets have become the sweethearts of the financial press and a favorite talking point of governments, foreign trade advisors, and corporations worldwide. Although these markets were best known in the past as a commodity paradise, or the place to go for natural resources, cheap labor, or low manufacturing costs, emerging markets today are positioned for growth. Rapid population development, growing middle-class, and sustained economic development are making many international investors and corporations look to emerging markets with new lenses.

Economic theorists' corroborate this point by arguing that free FDI across national borders is beneficial to all countries, as it leads to an efficient allocation of resources that raises productivity and economic growth everywhere. Although in principle this is often the case, at this time, for emerging markets, the situation is a bit different. It is much more apparent now, when we look at country indicators from sources such as the IMF or World Bank, that large capital inflows can create substantial challenges for policymakers in those market economies. After the global financial crisis of 2008 to 2009, net private capital flows to emerging markets surged and have been volatile since then. This raises a number of concerns in those recipient economies. As advanced economies issued robust monetary stimuli to revive their sluggish economies, emerging markets faced an overabundance of foreign investments amid strong recoveries. Hence, policy tensions rapidly ensued between these two groups of economies. As strong FDI, mainly private net capital, was injected into emerging markets economies, both in pre- and postglobal financial crisis periods, policymakers in those emerging economies reacted by actually reversing the flow of capital back into advanced market economies. This often resulted in an effort to control local currency appreciation, and fend off the exporting of inflation from advanced economies into these markets.

Therefore, we are all witnessing a rapid development in the global trade landscape, one that hitherto was dominated by advanced economies, with trading policies developed typically by members of the G-8 group of nations. Some members of the G-8 group though are beginning to lose their influence to emerging economies, as a result of profound changes the global markets are undergoing. One of the most important changes, henceforth the consequences of which still remain to be understood fully, is the growing role of the G-20 countries as new policymakers for international trade and fast developing emerging markets.

These groups of emerging economies, however, are not easy to define. While the World Bank coined the term *emerging countries* more than a quarter of a century ago, it only started to become a household term in the mid-1990s.* After the debt crises of the 1980s, several of these rapidly developing economies gained access to international financial markets, while at the same time they had liberalized their financial systems, at least far enough to enable foreign investors broad access into their markets.[1] From a small group of nations in East Asia, these groups of emerging economies have gradually grown to include several countries in Latin America, Central and Eastern Europe, and the Middle East, as well as a few countries in Africa. The leading groups today are the Association of South East Asian Nations (ASEAN), the BRICS, the CIVETS, and Middle East and North Africa (MENA), in addition to what Jim O'Neil calls the N-11, or Next-11 emerging economies, a focus of much discussion in this book.

---

* The term was coined in 1981 by Antoine W. van Agtmael of the International Finance Corporation of the World Bank, http://www.investopedia.com/articles/03/073003.asp, last accessed on October 29, 2013.

When studying emerging markets today, it is important to under-stand how the global economy is changing, what the world will look like tomorrow, five years from now, a decade from now, and how it will impact each of us. The weight of the emerging markets is already significant and being felt throughout the advanced economies and it is likely to expand further. The implications of the rise of the emerging markets on the world economy, some of which is already evident and will be discussed later in this chapter, cannot be disregarded by governance of the global economy organizations.

The Influence of Emerging Markets Across the Globe

The impact and influence of emerging markets on advanced economies and global trade is impressive. Today, these countries constitute over half of the world's population, with China and India accounting for over one third of it. As a result of intense economic transformations many of these emerging economies are facing rapid urbanization and industrialization. As of 2013, as shown in Figure 2.1, nine of the ten largest metropolitan areas in the world are located in emerging markets.

By 2050, the world's population is expected to grow by 2.3 billion people, reaching about 9.1 billion. By then most of the world's new mid-dle class will be living in the emerging economies of the world, and most of them in cities. Many of these cities have not yet been built, unless you count the plethora of ghost cities in China; cities built with the entire

Top 10 largest cities in the World 2013	
Emerging — Advanced	Population
10. Cairo, Egypt	19.6m
9. Sao Paulo, Brazil	19.8m
8. Shanghai, China	20.8m
7. Mexico City, Mexico	21.2m
6. Manila, Philippines	21.9m
5. New Delhi, India	22.2m
4. Seoul, South Korea	25.2m
3. Jakarta, Indonesia	28.0m
2. Chongqing, China	28.8m
1. Tokyo, Japan	35.1m

Figure 2.1 Top 10 largest cities in the world, 2013

Source: IMF World Outlook (2013).

necessary infrastructure. Physical infrastructure, such as water supply, sanitation and electricity systems, and soft infrastructure, such as recruitment agencies and intermediaries to deal with customer credit checks, will need to be built or upgraded to cope with the growing urban middle class.

As far as purchasing power, by 2030 the combined purchasing power of the global middle classes is estimated to more than double to $59 trillion. Most impressive, over 80 percent of this demand will come from Asia alone. That will come at a price though, as it will require an estimated $7.9 trillion in investments by 2020. Meeting these needs will likely entail public-private partnerships, new approaches to equity funding, and the development of capital markets.

Also impressive is the increasing size of these economies. The growth of economic strength of the BRIC countries alone is leading to greater power to influence world economic policy. Just recently, in October of 2010 emerging economies gained a greater voice under a breakthrough agreement that gave six percent of voting shares in the IMF to dynamic emerging countries such as China. As a result China became the IMF's third largest member. According to the IMF, and as depicted in Figure 2.2, by 2014 emerging markets are poised to overtake advanced economies in terms of share of global GDP.

As of 2013, as Figure 2.2 shows, emerging markets already account for about 50 percent of world's GDP and going forward, its contribution is

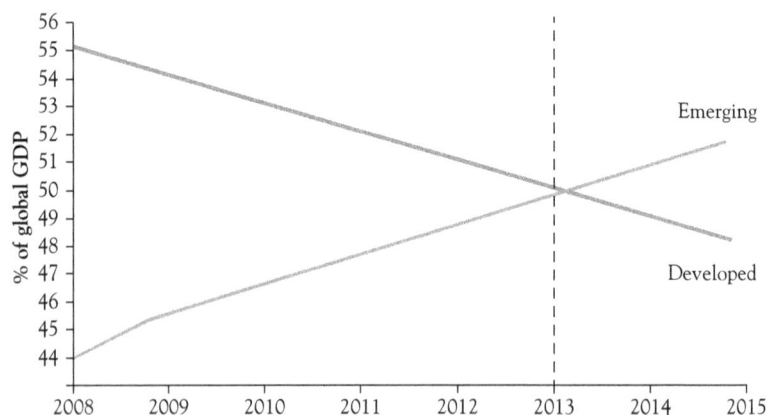

Figure 2.2 Advanced economies and emerging markets share of global GDP

Source: World Economic Outlook Database, International Monetary Fund, October 2010.

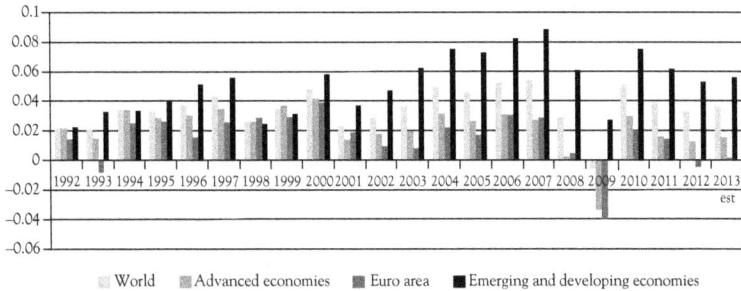

*Figure 2.3 **Emerging markets have driven global GDP growth for more than a decade***

Source: IMF.

expected to be higher than advanced economies. Not only are these economies enormous, but also they are growing exponentially. As Figure 2.2 also illustrates the divergence between the economic growth of emerging markets and advanced economies is projected to continue in the years to come. Figure 2.3 shows that since 2000, emerging markets have driven global GDP growth.

The data indicates that emerging markets are now one of the main engines of world growth. As a result, emerging countries' citizens have reaped the benefits of such rapid development with higher standards of living, fostering the growth of a huge middle-class with discretionary income to spend in goods and services, and thus impacting advanced economies in a very positive way.

These billions of new middle class consumers in the emerging markets represent new markets for advanced economies' exports and multinational corporations based in developed countries. Ford Motor Company, for example, draws almost 47 percent of its revenues from foreign markets, mainly from emerging markets. Also, strong growth in emerging markets increases the demand for those goods and tradable services where the advanced economies have comparative advantages.

According to the Economist Intelligence Unit the change in real GDP per capita in emerging markets has significantly surpassed that of advanced economies. Figure 2.4 shows a striking contrast. As of 2011 per capita GDP has risen substantially faster in many emerging market countries as compared to advanced economies. The top 10 are all emerging

Change in Real GDP per person fourth quarter 2007 through second quarter 2011

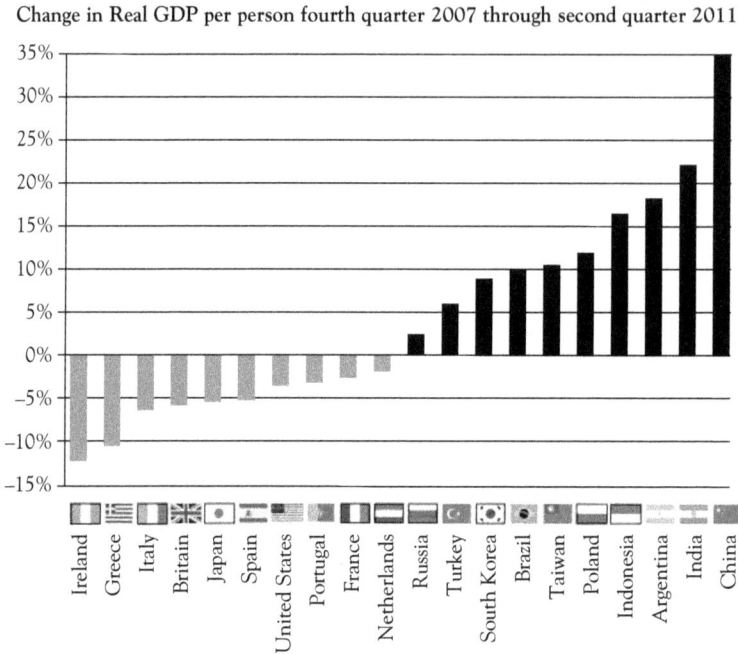

Figure 2.4 The change in real GDP per capita in emerging markets has surpassed advanced economies by far

markets in Asia, South America, and Eastern Europe. China topped the world with nearly a 35 percent change in real GDP per person, followed by India, which had a rate change of more than 20 percent. Argentina and Brazil also grew significantly, as did Poland, Turkey, and Russia. Advanced economies, however, are debt-burdened and have detracted. Ireland and Greece have declined more than 10 percent. During the same period, the United States had the seventh worst change in real GDP per capita.

These are fairly known macroeconomic facts. Perhaps even more striking is the microeconomic evidence of the economic success of emerging markets in the last decade and beyond. For instance, according to Forbes' Global 2000 ranking, four out of the 20 largest companies in the world, in terms of market value, are from emerging markets.[2] From these four companies, two oil and gas firms, one Russian (Gazprom) and one Chinese (PetroChina) rank among the top 10. Also according to Forbes,[3] seven of the 24 richest individuals in the world are from the emerging markets, including Carlos Slim Helu (3rd), from Mexico; Li Ka-shing (9th) from Hong Kong; Prince Alwaleed Bin Talal Alsaud (13th), from

Saudi Arabia; Mukesh Ambani (14th) from India; Anil Ambani (18th) also from India; Azim Premji (21st) from India; and Lee Shau Kee (22nd) from Hong Kong.

If the present looks promising for emerging market economies, their potential future seems even brighter. According to available projections for long-term growth, based on demographic trends and models of capital accumulation and productivity, emerging markets are likely to become even more prominent in the world economy looking forward than they are today. Of course, political instabilities need to be accounted for, especially in the short term for some of these countries facing political turmoil. Nonetheless, a number of studies offer startling data regarding the growth prospects of emerging markets. According to a study by Wilson and Purushothaman[4] (2003), by 2025 the BRIC countries could account for over half the size of today's six largest economies; in less than 40 years, they could be even larger. Other studies, such as Hawksworth[5] and Poncet,[6] convey similar messages, notwithstanding some nominal differences.

Emerging market leaders are expected to become a disruptive force in the global competitive landscape. As emerging market countries gain in stature, new multinational companies (MNCs) will continue to take center stage in global markets. The rise of these emerging MNCs as market leaders will constitute one of the fastest-growing global trends of this decade and beyond. These MNCs will continue to be critical competitors in their home markets while increasingly making outbound investments into other emerging and advanced economies.

Many emerging market leaders have grown up in markets with *institutional voids*, where support systems such as retail distribution channels, reliable transportation and telecommunications systems, and adequate water supply simply don't exist. Physical infrastructure, such as water supply, sanitation and electricity systems, and soft infrastructure, such as recruitment agencies and intermediaries to deal with customer credit checks, are still being developed, if they exist at all, in order to cope with the growing urban middle class.

Addressing such concerns will require several trillions of dollars in investments by 2020, which could be very good news for advanced economies and professionals with an eye on and expertise with international businesses. Meeting these needs will likely entail public-private partnerships, new approaches to equity funding, and the development of capital markets.

Having learned to overcome the challenges of serving customers of limited means in their own domestic markets, these emerging MNC market leaders are already developing and producing innovative designs, while reducing manufacturing costs and often disrupting entire industries around the world. As a result, these companies possess a more innovative, entrepreneurial culture and have developed greater flexibility to meet the demands of their local and *bottom-of-the-pyramid* customers.

The developments we observe today, with the rapid rising of emerging markets outpacing advanced economies, are likely to be the precursor of a profound rebalancing in the distribution of world output in the very near future. Of course, it cannot be excluded that this process might well be "nonlinear," with episodes of discontinuity, perhaps also including financial crises somewhere down the line.

The Influences of the ASEAN Bloc

Many emerging market countries that previously posed no competitive threat to advanced economies now do. The financial crisis that started in mid-1997 in Southeast Asia, and resulted in massive currency depreciations in a number of emerging markets in that region, spilled over to many other emerging nations as far as Latin America and Africa. But such crisis since then has subsided, as these same regions were the first to recover from the latest crisis of 2008. The intense currency depreciation in Asia during the late 90s has positioned the region for a more competitive landscape across global markets.

According to an Organization for Economic Cooperation and Development (OECD) report[7] and as depicted in Figure 2.5,* although these emerging market economies in Asia have experienced massive exchange rate depreciations, they also have reinforced their absolute cost advantages given the increasing importance of these economies in world trade. Countries such as Thailand, Indonesia, and South Korea, which were impacted the most during the 1990s are now emerging market

---

* Source: http://www.oecd.org/eco/outlook/2088912.pdf

Percent[a]			
	vis-à-vis U.S. dollar	vis-à-vis Japanese yen	vis-à-vis Deutsche mark
China	0	13	5
Chinese Taipei	−15	−3	10
Hong Kong, China	0	13	5
Indonesia	−76	−73	−75
Korea	−40	−32	−37
Malaysia	−32	−22	−28
Philippines	−32	−24	−29
Singapore	11	1	7
Thailand	−40	−32	−37

a = Changes between July 1, 1997, and March 18, 1998.

Figure 2.5 Changes in Asian emerging market economies exchange rates since mid-1997

leaders, representing a major shift in the global competitive landscape. We believe this is a trend that will continue to strengthen as these countries grow in size, establish dominance, and seek new opportunities beyond their traditional domestic and near-shore markets.

Meanwhile, advanced economies in the G-7 group are still struggling with indebtedness. The United States continues to deal with debt ceiling adjustments to cope with its everincreasing government debt while the eurozone is far from solving its own economic problems. Conversely, despite inevitable risks and uncertainties, Southeast Asia registered solid economic growth in 2012 and continues to be on an upward trajectory for the foreseeable future, as China's economy stabilizes and higher levels of foreign direct investment (FDI) are pouring in.

The ASEAN is an organization of countries located in the Southeast Asian region that aims to accelerate economic growth, social progress, and cultural development among its members and to promote regional peace. The region has undergone a period of substantial resurgence after the 1997 through 1998 Asian financial crises and has been playing second fiddle to more industrialized economies in Asia-Pacific, which manage to attract the majority of capital inflows. What we've seen since the financial crisis, however, is that ASEAN has been showcasing its ability to recover and advance its position within global markets.

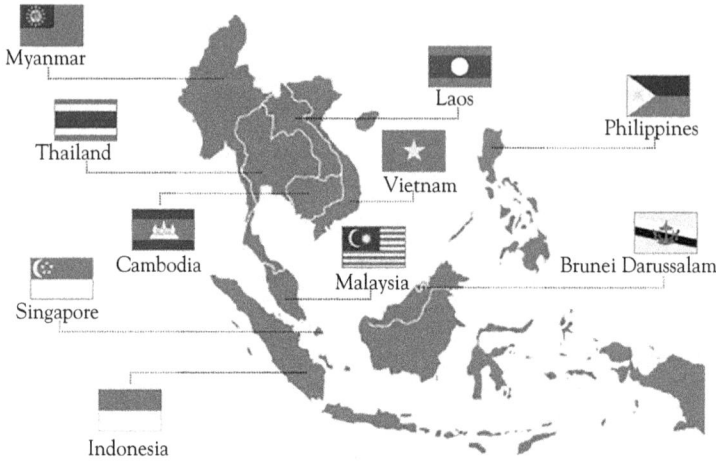

Figure 2.6 List of ASEAN member countries as of 2012[8]

Source: ASEAN.

As of 2012, the ASEAN bloc is comprised of ten member states including Brunei Darussalam, Cambodia, Indonesia, Laos PDR, Malaysia, Myanmar, Philippines, Singapore, Thailand, and Vietnam, as shown in Figure 2.6.

Studies carried out by the Asian Development Bank Institute (ADBI)[9] suggests that the emergence of international production networks in East Asia results from market-driven forces such as vertical specialization and higher production costs in the home countries and institutional-led initiatives, such as free trade agreements. For instance, the region has experienced significant growth in the trade of parts and components since the 1990s, especially with China, who is one of the important major assembly bases. In addition, the decline in the share of parts and components trade in several members of the ASEAN bloc, such as Indonesia and Thailand, indicates the increasing importance of the bloc countries as assembly bases for advanced economies such as Japan, and its multinational enterprises (MNEs). China and Thailand are becoming important auto parts assembly bases for Japan and other advanced economies, attracting foreign investments into those countries, raising their GDP and contributing more to the emergence of international production networks than just free trade agreements. Figure 2.7 provides a list of ASEAN members

Rank ⬍	Country ⬍	Population in millions ⬍		GDP Nominal millions of USD ⬍		GDP Nominal per capita USD ⬍		GDP (PPP) millions of USD ⬍		GDP (PPP) per capita USD ⬍	
—	World	7,013.42		71,707,302		10,200		83,140,055		11,850	
—	European Union	502.56		16,584,007		32,518		16,092,525		32,021	
—	United States	314.18		15,684,750		49,922		15,684,750		49,922	
—	China	1,354.04		8,227,037		6,076		12,405,670		9,162	
—	Japan	127.61		5,963,969		46,736		4,627,891		36,266	
—	ASEAN	615.60	100.0	2,305,542	100.0	3,745	100.0	3,605,602	100.0	5,857	100.0
—	South Korea	50.01		1,155,872		23,113		1,613,921		32,272	
1	Indonesia	244.47	39.7	878,198	38.1	3,592	95.9	1,216,738	33.7	4,977	85.0
2	Thailand	64.38	10.5	365,564	15.9	5,678	151.6	651,856	18.1	10,126	172.9
3	Malaysia	29.46	4.8	303,527	13.2	10,304	275.1	498,477	13.8	16,922	288.9
4	Singapore	5.41	0.9	276,520	12.0	51,162	1,366.1	326,506	9.1	60,410	1,031.4
5	Philippines	95.80	15.6	250,436	10.9	2,614	69.8	424,355	11.8	4,430	75.6
6	Vietnam	90.39	14.7	138,071	6.0	1,528	40.8	320,677	8.9	3,548	60.6
7	Myanmar	63.67	10.3	53,140	2.3	835	22.3	89,461	2.5	1,405	24.0
8	Brunei	0.40	0.1	16,628	0.7	41,703	1,113.5	21,687	0.6	54,389	928.6
9	Cambodia	15.25	2.5	14,241	0.6	934	24.9	36,645	1.0	2,402	41.0
10	Laos	6.38	1.0	9,217	0.4	1,446	38.6	19,200	0.5	3,011	51.4

Figure 2.7 List of ASEAN countries GDP

Source: IMF Global Outlook (2012), estimates.

and their respective GDP, as well as a comparison with major G-7 member states, with exception to China.

Of course, the ASEAN region has had its fair share of risks and challenges, which unfortunately are not going away. ASEAN politicians, like politicians everywhere, occasionally cave in to populist measures. Since the crises of 2008, these populist measures have been present in both the advanced economies and emerging markets, with only the level of intensity as the single variant. But ASEAN's deep commitment to macroeconomic stability, open trade, business-friendly policies, and regional cooperation has created the foundation for steady growth in those regions.

This is also true for many emerging market nations around the globe and in particular the BRICS. Nonetheless, the ASEAN region remains among the most attractive destination for foreign investors who are running out of options in other emerging markets. Its relative political and macroeconomic stability, low levels of debt, integration in East Asian production networks, and open trade and investment policies are giving the region a distinct advantage over other emerging markets around the

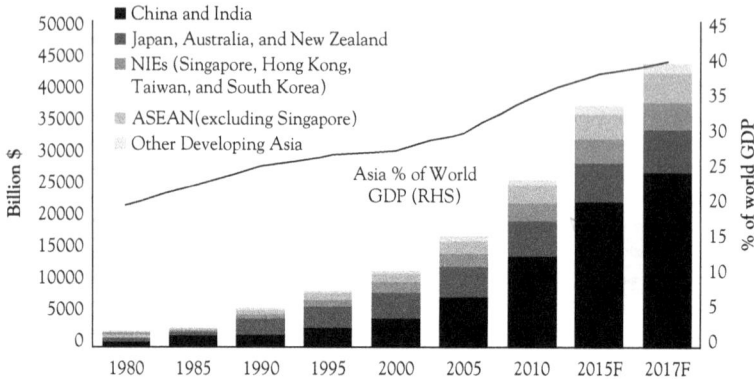

Figure 2.8 Asian Economic GDP growth based on purchasing power parity

Note: F-Forecasted.

world. As depicted in Figure 2.8, these countries have been growing at an average rate above six percent (in 2012) a year, with Indonesia and the Philippines exceeding GDP forecasts. Thailand, hit with devastating floods in 2011 has now recovered and is in full swing to achieve higher than expected GDP growth. The same goes for Malaysia, which has enjoyed the benefits of an expansionary election budget.

According to Arno Maierbrugger, from Investvine,[10] the ASEAN economy will more than double by 2020, with the nominal GDP of the regional bloc increasing from $2 trillion in 2012 to $4.7 trillion. The global research firm IHS[11] argues that Vietnam and Myanmar are expected to reach a nominal GDP of $290 billion and $103 billion, respectively, by 2020, while Indonesia is expected to reach a projected nominal GDP of about $1.9 trillion. The report also says that overall, emerging markets in Asia are expected to be the fastest growing in the world and will continue to expand. It estimated that GDP growth of emerging markets would exceed that of developed countries in 2020, continuing to expand thereafter.

Internal macroeconomic policies and structural reforms in the ASEAN region will continue to drive growth in the foreseeable future. The Philippines and Myanmar should see higher GDP growth as a result of earnest government efforts to improve economic governance. Myanmar, after 50 years of self-imposed isolation, fear, and poverty, has rejoined the international community, attracting fresh foreign investments, which should yield significant growth dividends.

In 2013, two parallel efforts toward trade integration, the ASE-AN-driven Regional Comprehensive Economic Partnership (RCEP) and the U.S.-driven TPP, began vying for traction beyond the ASEAN bloc. Currently, the TPP is more advanced but faces important challenges before it can come to closure. Discussions on the RCEP have only just begun and also face significant obstacles, but progress could accelerate if an agreement on the basic parameters is reached soon. Although both of these trade agreements should be able to coexist, they not only include a set of advanced economies, which can be very beneficial to those countries, but also represent different philosophies as to how economic integration should be achieved.

The risk to emerging markets in the ASEAN bloc and the advanced economies partnership in trade, as in TTP, are the mounting tensions in the South China Sea, with China facing off against Vietnam and the Philippines. ASEAN's diplomatic attempts to defuse the conflict have only succeeded in raising them even further. It is important now that under a new chair in Brunei, ASEAN countries find ways to settle their internal differences, agree quickly on a code of conduct for the South China Sea, and engage China early in the process so that it becomes an important stakeholder in its implementation and international trade.

Despite geopolitical risks in the region, one of the major catalysts for ASEAN's accelerated growth is its relative specialized low labor costs. While estimates of cost levels in the manufacturing sector are not fully available, data from OECD and the IMF suggest that over the 1975 to 1996 period, China (including Taipei) and South Korea in particular were able to maintain significantly lower levels of specialized labor costs than any other industrialized countries for which data exist. Important to note, as argued by Durant et al.[12] (1998) is the fact that while in the past these potential competitive advantages deriving from nominal exchange rate depreciations often tended to be eroded by rising inflation, there is a widespread sentiment that recent global economic and in-country financial policy developments might have reinforced the absolute cost advantage that emerging markets already might have compared to OECD countries, which makes these markets even more competitive internationally.

Such arguments are reinforced by the fact that, in principle, competitiveness is normally correlated with companies, which can gain and lose market shares, and eventually even go out of business. The same cannot be said for countries. As P. Krugman (1996) argues,[13] countries cannot go out of business and therefore we should not care about competing countries. Nonetheless, in our opinion, countries still need to be concerned with shifts in market shares, since such shifts may indicate changes in the composition of country output and in the living standards of that nation. Hence, it is likely that labor cost levels in most other emerging market economies in the ASEAN bloc also are much lower, than in other nations, particularly advanced economies, as depicted in Figure 2.9.

We believe leading emerging markets will continue to drive global growth. Estimates show that 70 percent of world growth over the next decade, well into 2020 and beyond, will come from emerging markets, with China and India accounting for 40 percent of that growth. Such

	USA = 100		
	1985	**1990**	**1996**
United States	100	100	100
Japan	74	116	169
Germany[a]	71	144	166
France	96	154	163
Italy	60	114	101
United Kingdom	100	158	148
Canada	84	118	102
Australia	98	118	145
Belgium	75	135	156
Denmark	97	205	218
Korea	29	51	58
Netherlands	65	122	120
Spain	49	108	100
Sweden	82	158	160
Chinese Taipei	41	70	70

Figure 2.9 Relative levels of unit labor costs in manufacturing

[a]*West Germany.*
Source: OECD calculations based on 1990 PPPs. For details on the methodological aspects, see OECD (1993).

growth is even more significant if we look at it from the purchasing power parity (PPP) perspective, which, adjusted for variation, the IMF forecasts that the total GDP of emerging markets could overtake that of advanced economies as early as 2014. Such forecasts also suggest that FDI will continue to find its way into emerging markets, particularly the ASEAN bloc, but also to the fast-developing MENA bloc, as well as Africa as a whole, followed by the BRIC and CIVETS. In all, however, the emerging markets already attract almost 50 percent of FDI global inflows and account for 25 percent of FDI outflows.

As noted earlier, between now and 2050, the world's population is expected to grow by 2.3 billion people, eventually reaching 9.1 billion. The combined purchasing power of the global middle classes is estimated to more than double by 2030 to $56 trillion. Over 80 percent of this demand will come from Asia. Most of the world's new middle class will live in the emerging world, and almost all will live in cities, often in smaller cities not yet built. This surge of urbanization will stimulate business but put huge strains on infrastructure.

The Influences of the BRICS Bloc

The original BRIC countries included Brazil, Russia, India, and China. Jim O'Neill, a retired former asset manager at Goldman and Sachs, coined the acronym back in 2001 in his paper entitled *Building Better Global Economic BRICs*.[14] The acronym came into widespread use as a symbol of the apparent shift in global economic power away from the developed G-7 economies toward the emerging markets. When we look at the size of its economies in GDP terms, however, the order of the letters in the acronym changes, with China leading the way (second in the world), followed by Brazil (sixth), India (ninth), and Russia (tenth).* In 2010 despite the lack of support from leading economists participating at the Reuters 2011 Investment Outlook Summit,[15] South Africa (28th) joined the BRIC bloc, forming a new acronym dubbed BRICS.[16]

It has been difficult to project future influences of the BRICS on the global economy. While some research suggests this bloc might overtake the

---

* According to United Nations 2011 ranking.

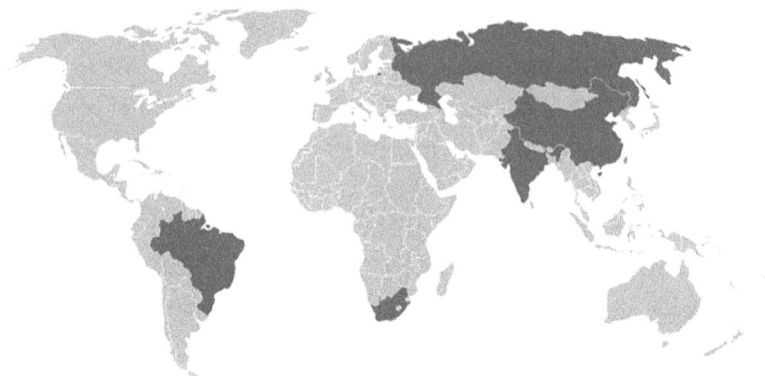

Figure 2.10 The BRICS countries: Brazil, Russia, India, China, and South Africa

G-7 economies by 2027,[17] other more modest forecasts, such as Goldman Sachs, argue that while the BRICS are developing rapidly, their combined economies could eclipse the combined economies of the current richest countries of the world by 2050.[18] In his recent book titled *The Growth Map: Economic Opportunity in the BRICs and Beyond*,[19] O'Neil corrects his earlier forecast by arguing the BRICS may overtake the G-7 by 2035. Such forecast represents an amazing accomplishment considering how disparate some of these countries are from each other geographically and the differences in their culture and political and religious systems. Figure 2.10 illustrates the BRICS geographical locations on the globe.

Notwithstanding these uncertain economic forecasts, researchers seem to agree that the BRICS have a major impact on their regional trading partners, more distant resource-rich countries, and in particular advanced economies. The ascent of these formerly impoverished countries is gaining momentum, and their confidence is evident. Former Chinese Premier Wen Jiabao stated in 2009 that China had "loaned huge amounts of money," to the United States, warning the United States and others to "honor its word" and "ensure the safety of Chinese assets." The Prime Minister of India, Manmohan Singh, has blamed the "massive failure" of the global financial system in 2008 on authorities in "developed societies," but his peers all name the United States by name. Vladimir Putin, the fourth president of Russia scorns "the irresponsibility of the system that claims leadership," while Luiz Inácio Lula da Silva, former President

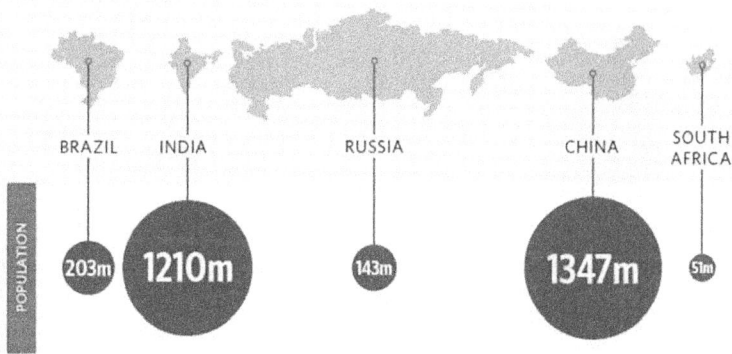

Figure 2.11 **BRICS** *account for almost 50 percent of world population*

Source: Population Reference Bureau.

of Brazil, in an interview with *Newsweek* magazine during the G-20 Summit in London, said the United States bears the brunt of responsibility for the crisis, and for fixing it.[20]

No doubt, there is a lot of global macroeconomics synergy behind the BRICS, and the performance indicators are backing it up. As of 2012, these countries accounted for over a quarter of the world's land mass and more than 46 percent of the world's population,[21] as depicted in Figure 2.11, although still only accounting for 25 percent of the world GDP.[22] Nonetheless, by 2020, this bloc of countries is expected to account for nearly 50 percent of all global GDP growth.

Since its formation, it is clear the BRICS have been seeking to form a *political club*. According to a Reuter's article, the BRIC bloc has strong interest in converting "their growing economic power into greater geopolitical clout."[23] Granted, the BRICS bloc does not represent a political coalition currently capable of playing a leading geopolitical role on the global stage. That being said, over the last decade the BRICS has come to symbolize the growing power of the world's largest emerging economies and their potential impact on the global economic and, increasingly, political order. All BRICS countries are current members of the United Nations Security Council. Russia and China are permanent members with veto power, while Brazil, India, and South Africa are nonpermanent members currently serving on the Council. Furthermore, the combined BRICS hold less than 15 percent of voting rights in both the World Bank

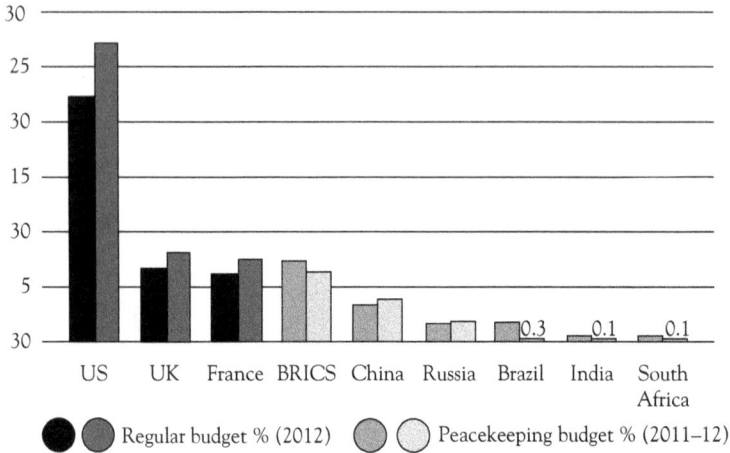

Figure 2.12 **BRICS have increased their participation and contribution to UN budgets**

and the IMF, yet still their economies are predicted to surpass the G-7 economies in size by 2032. This can only strengthen their position at the UN, IMF, and the World Bank.

As depicted in Figure 2.12, BRICS have stepped up their participation in the United Nations by donating large sums of money to its regular and peacekeeping budgets. Russia has gone ahead and led the bloc by holding the firm BRIC summit back in June of 2009 in Yekaterinburg, issuing a declaration calling for the establishment of an equitable, democratic, and multipolar world order.[24] Since then, according to the Times,[25] the BRICS have met in Brasília, Brazil (2010), in Sanya, China (2011), and in New Delhi, India (2012).

In recent years, the BRICs have received increasing scholarly attention. Brazilian political economist Marcos Troyjo and French investment banker Christian Déséglise founded the BRICLab at Columbia University, a forum examining the strategic, political, and economic consequences of the rise of BRIC countries, especially by analyzing their projects for power, prosperity, and prestige through graduate courses, special sessions with guest speakers, Executive Education programs, and annual conferences for policymakers, business and academic leaders, and students.[26]

The Challenge of Global Influence

The BRICS' continuing growing economic strength is advancing toward greater power to influence world economic policy. In October 2010, for example, emerging economies gained a greater voice under a landmark agreement that gave six percent of IMF voting shares to dynamic emerging countries such as China. Under this agreement, China will become the IMF's third-largest member.

The differences between the BRIC bloc, in terms of values, economics, political structure, and geopolitical interests, far outweigh the commonalities. There are, however, fundamental commonalities, particularly with regard to mild anti-Americanism, and the overall internal and domestic challenges these countries face, including institutional stability, social inequality, and demographic pressures. The BRICS bloc is important for members in terms of the symbolism of creating for themselves an important role on the global stage, with a desire to wield greater influence over the rules governing international commerce, and economic policy.

Castro Neves, a founding partner at CAC Political Consultancy, and also contributing editor at *The Brazilian Economy* magazine, argues that Brazil's "foreign policy priority is to consolidate its economic gains at the national level by building international influence and partners, and the BRICS group represents an important opportunity to realize that vision."[27] Fyodor Lukyanov, Editor of Global Affairs in Moscow, Russia, believes the bloc, although "unable to take a concerted stand on the new head of the IMF," has an opportunity "to have a more influential, if not major, global role in the future."*

We believe the absence of shared values between all BRICS members limits the global potential for the bloc. The inclusion of South Africa to the group may have been a good strategy, but the pull toward expanding the group to new members would dilute any cohesiveness it currently possesses.

The Influences of the CIVETS Bloc

The CIVETS acronym, which includes Colombia, Indonesia, Vietnam, Egypt, Turkey, and South Africa, as illustrated in Figure 2.13, was coined

---

* Ibidem.

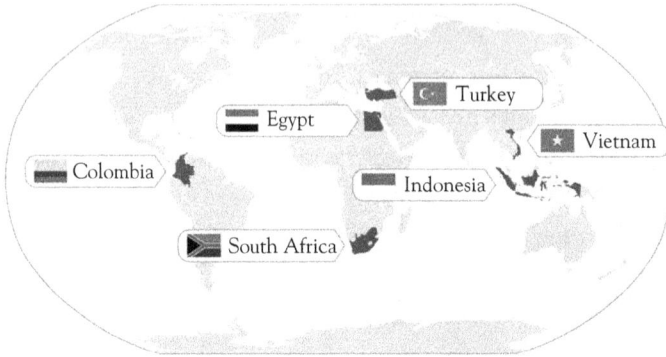

Figure 2.13 The CIVETS bloc

by Robert Ward, Global Director of the Global Forecasting Team of the Economist Intelligence Unit (EIU) in late 2009.[28] It was then further circulated by Michael Geoghegan, President of the Anglo-Chinese HSBC bank, in a speech to the Hong Kong Chamber of Commerce in April 2010. These groups of countries are predicted to be among the next emerging markets to quickly rise in economic prominence over the coming decades for their relative political stability, young populations that focus on education, and overall growing economic trends. Geoghegan compared these countries to the civet, a carnivorous mammal that eats and partially digests coffee cherries, passing a transformed coffee bean that fetches high prices.

The CIVETS bloc is about 10 years younger than the BRICS with similar characteristics. All of these bloc countries are growing very quickly and have relatively diverse economies. They offer a greater advantage over the BRICS, as they don't depend as heavily on foreign demands. They also have reasonably sophisticated financial systems, controlled inflation, and soaring young populations with fast-rising domestic consumption.[29]

Geoghegan argued in 2010 that emerging markets would grow three times as fast as developed countries that year, suggesting that the center of gravity of the world growth and economic development was moving toward Asia and Latin America.* All the CIVETS countries, except Colombia and South Africa, also are part of O'Neil's Next Eleven (N-11) countries. As depicted in Figure 2.14, this includes Bangladesh, Egypt, Indonesia, Iran,

---

* Ibidem.

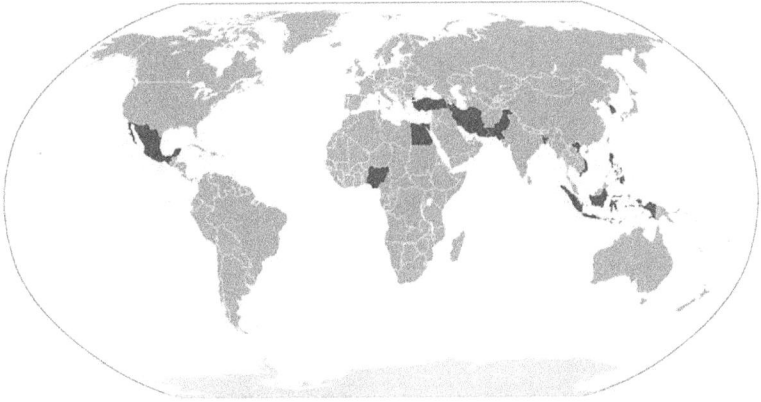

Figure 2.14 The Next-Eleven (N-11) countries

Mexico, Nigeria, Pakistan, Philippines, Turkey, South Korea, and Vietnam. These countries are believed to have a high chance of becoming, along with the BRICS, the world's largest economies in the 21st century.[30]

Some critics argue that the CIVETS countries have nothing in common beyond their youth populations. What does Egypt have in common with Vietnam? Data also suggest that on the negative side, liquidity and corporate governance are patchy, while political risks remain a factor, as seen with Egypt in the past few years.

The Influences of the MENA Countries

According to the World Bank,[31] the bloc, commonly known as MENA covers an extensive region, extending from Morocco to Iran and including the majority of both the Middle Eastern and Maghreb countries. The World Bank argues that due to the geographic ambiguity and Eurocentric nature of the term *Middle East*, people often prefer to use the term WANA (West Asia and North Africa)* or the less common NAWA (North Africa-West Asia), as argued by Shlomit et al.[32] As depicted in Figure 2.15, MENA countries include Algeria, Bahrain, Djibouti, Egypt, Iran, Iraq, Israel, Jordan, Kuwait, Lebanon, Libya, Malta, Morocco, Oman, Qatar, Saudi Arabia, North and South Sudan, Syria, Tunisia, United Arab Emirates (UAE), Yemen, West Bank, and Gaza.

---

* http://www.worldbank.org/html/cgiar/newsletter/april97/8beltagy.html

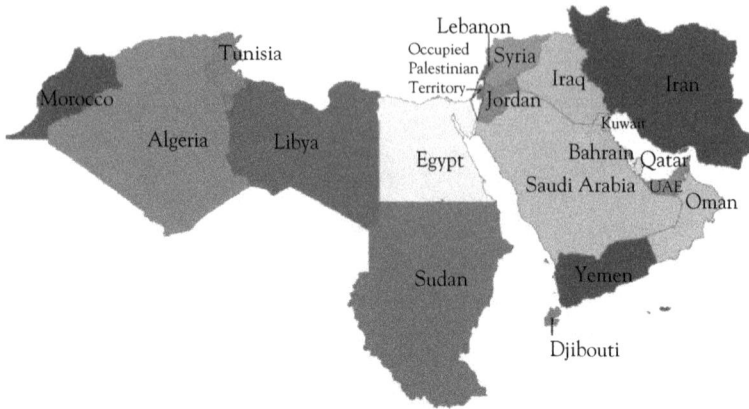

Figure 2.15 The MENA countries (dark shade) and other countries often considered as part of the bloc (lighter shade)

Source: GreenProfit.

The MENA bloc, regardless if known as WANA or NAWA (we'll be using MENA throughout this book), is an economically diverse region that includes both the oil-rich economies in the Gulf and countries that are resource-scarce in relation to population, such as Egypt, Morocco, and Yemen. According to the Middle East Strategy at Harvard (MESH) project at the John Olin Institute for Strategic Study at Harvard University, the population of the MENA region, as depicted in Figure 2.16, at its least extent is roughly 381 million people, about six percent of the total world population. At its greatest extent, its population is roughly 523 million.

Two years after the *Arab Spring* commenced, many nations in the MENA region are still undergoing complex political, social, and economic transitions. Economic performance indicators were mixed in 2012, while most of the oil-exporting countries grew at healthy rates; the same is not true for oil importing ones, which have been growing at a sluggish pace. However, due to the scaling-back of hydrocarbon production among oil exporters and a mild economic recovery among oil importers, the differences narrowed in 2013. In all, many of these countries are confronted with the immediate challenge of re-establishing or sustaining macroeconomic stability amid political uncertainty and social

Population size and growth in the countries of the Middle East and North Africa: 1950, 2007, and 2050					
	Population in thousands			Ratio of population	
Country and region	1950	2007	2050*	2007/ 1950	2050/ 2007
Middle East and North Africa (MENA)	103,886	431,578	692,299	4.2	1.6
MENA-Western Asia	51,452	215,976	332,081	4.2	1.5
Iran	16,913	71,208	100,174	4.2	1.4
Iraq	5,340	28,993	61,942	5.4	2.1
Israel	1,258	6,928	10,527	5.5	1.5
Jordan	472	5,924	10,121	12.5	1.7
Lebanon	1,443	4,099	5,221	2.8	1.3
Palestinian Territory	1,005	4,017	10,265	4.0	2.6
Syria	3,536	19,929	34,887	5.6	1.8
Turkey	21,484	74,877	98,946	3.5	1.3
Arabian Peninsula	8,336	58,544	123,946	7.0	2.1
Bahrain	116	753	1,173	6.5	1.6
Kuwait	152	2,851	5,240	18.7	1.8
Oman	456	2,595	4,639	5.7	1.8
Qatar	25	841	1,333	33.6	1.6
Saudi Arabia	3,201	24,735	45,030	7.7	1.8
United Arab Emirates	70	4,380	8,521	62.9	1.9
Yemen	4,316	22,389	58,009	5.2	2.6
Northern Africa	44,099	157,068	236,272	3.6	1.5
Algeria	8,753	33,858	49,610	3.9	1.5
Egypt	21,834	75,498	121,219	3.5	1.6
Morocco	8,953	31,224	42,583	3.5	1.4
Libya	1,029	6,160	9,683	6.0	1.6
Tunisia	3,530	10,327	13,178	2.9	1.3

Figure 2.16 MENA's population size and growth (MESH)

*Projected
Source: UN Population Division. World Population Prospects: The 2006 Revision (2007; http://esa.un.org/, accessed April 10, 2007): table A.2.

unrest, but the region must not lose sight of the medium-term challenge of diversifying its economies, creating jobs, and generating more inclusive growth.

The region's economic wealth over much of the past quarter century has been heavily influenced by two factors: the price of oil and the legacy of economic policies and structures that had emphasized a leading role for the state. With about 23 percent of the 300 million people in the Middle East and North Africa living on less than two dollars a day, however, empowering poor people constitutes an important strategy for fighting poverty.

Modest growth is anticipated, however, across the region. According to the IMF,[33] subdued growth in MENA oil importers is expected to improve in 2013, although such growth is not expected to be sufficient to even begin making sizable inroads into the region's large unemployment problem. The external environment continues to exert pressure on international reserves in many oil-importing countries among the MENA bloc and remains a challenge. In addition, sluggish economic activity with trading partners, mostly advanced economies, in particular the eurozone area, is holding back a quicker recovery of exports. Elevated commodity prices continue to weigh on external balances in countries that depend on food and energy imports. Tourist arrivals, which have decreased significantly since the terrorist attacks on the United States in 2001, are gradually rebounding, but remain well below pre-2011 levels and before the global recession set in.

According to a new study reported in the Dubai-based Khaleej Times,[34] the sunny region and its associated countries could solar power the world three times over. If such projections ever become reality, poverty may have a chance to be eradicated in the region. Countries that move fast, the study suggests, could have the competitive advantage. MENA countries, especially ones located on the Arabian Peninsula, as well as others like Jordan, Lebanon, and Israel are well positioned to take the lead in this industry. These countries are no strangers to the notion of solar energy. As the Khaleej Times article points out the countries in the MENA region have the "greatest potential for solar regeneration" supplying 45 percent of the world's energy sources possible through renewable energy. Renewable energy sources of interest in this region include Abu

Real GDP growth rates (%)

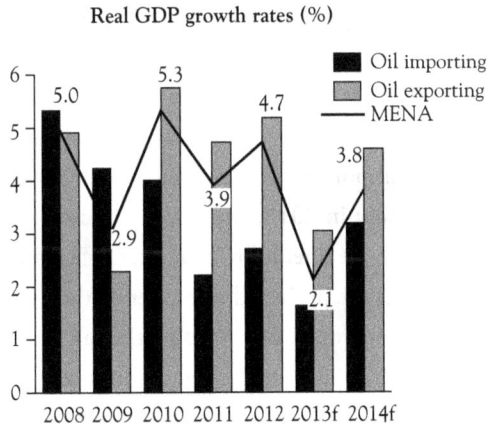

Figure 2.17 MENA's real GDP growth rates

Dhabi's Masdar City as well as its hosting of the World Renewable Energy Agency headquarters.

Funding for these projects may pose an issue. Foreign direct investment, according to the IMF,[35] is expected to remain restrained and lower than in other emerging markets and advanced economies. Moreover, growing regional economic and social spillovers from the conflict in Syria is expected to add to the complexity of MENA's economic environment. While oil-exporting countries, mainly in the Gulf Cooperation Council (GCC), face a more positive outlook, there is still the risk of a worsening of the global economic outlook, particularly with advanced economies, which are major consumers of oil. Should this occur, oil exporting nations within MENA will likely face serious economic pressures. A prolonged decline in oil prices, rooted in persistently low global economic activity, for instance, could run down reserve buffers and result in fiscal deficits for the region.

The latest IMF's World Economic Outlook* projections suggest that economic performance in the MENA bloc will remain mixed. According to Qatar National Bank Group (QNB Group),[36] this dual speed development should continue over the next few years, with the GCC countries as the driving force for growth in the MENA region and the main source of investment and financing. As shown in Figure 2.17, the Group

---

* http://www.imf.org/external/pubs/ft/weo/2013/01/ last accessed on 11/02/2013.

forecasts MENA's economy to grow 2.1 percent in 2013 and 3.8 percent in 2014. Note in Figure 2.17 that the overall forecast disguises a significant difference in performance between oil exporters, including the GCC countries, and oil importers. The 2012 restrained growth of 2.7 percent in MENA oil importers is expected to fall to 1.6 percent in 2013 and recover to 3.2 percent in 2014, which will not create enough jobs to reduce these countries' large unemployment rates. Meanwhile, oil exporters' healthy growth rates are projected to moderate this year to three percent as they scale back increases in oil production amidst modest global energy demand. Continued large infrastructure investment is expected to lead to a rise in economic growth to 4.5 percent in 2014.

In addition, the MENA countries in transition continue to face political uncertainty with the challenge of delivering on the expectations for jobs and fostering economic cohesion, which also deters growth. In particular, the Syrian crisis has had a strong negative impact on growth in the Mashreq region—the region of Arab countries to the east of Egypt and north of the Arabian Peninsula, such as Iraq, Palestine and Israel, Jordan, Kuwait, Lebanon, and Syria. Syria has a large amount of refugees straining the fiscal resources of countries like Iraq, Jordan, Lebanon, and, to a lesser extent, Turkey. A notable example is the more than 800,000 Syrian refugees who have already entered Lebanon, about 19 percent of the population, and have had a substantial impact on the already weak fiscal position of the Lebanese budget. Equally damaging have been the setbacks of the political transitions as well as the escalation of violence in Libya, Egypt, and Tunisia, which have further deterred FDI and much needed economic reforms.

Looking ahead, MENA countries will continue on their path of economic transition owing primarily to the benign GCC outlook, which will continue to act as the locomotive for regional growth. That said, caution must be given to the external environment in volatile oil importing countries with spillovers from the Syria conflict. Finally, as important as it is now to focus on maintaining economic stability, it is critical for MENA governments not to lose sight of the fundamental medium-term challenge of modernizing and diversifying the region's economies, creating more jobs, and providing fair and equitable opportunities for all.

CHAPTER 3

Advanced Versus Emerging Markets

Global Economic Prospects

Overview

Advanced economies and emerging markets find themselves in different economic and political cycles, which are causing the global recovery to ascend at two different speeds. In 2011, the IMF estimated the global economy was growing at 4.4 percent, while advanced economies were growing at 2.4 percent and emerging markets at 6.5 percent. However, according to most recent data (2014), the IMF predicts a slowdown in growth, expecting the global economy to grow at 3.6 percent (3.9 percent in 2015), while advanced economies will grow at 2.25 percent in 2014–2015, and emerging markets at 5 percent (5 ¼ percent for 2015).

The global economic growth trend is changing significantly. Emerging markets were responsible for roughly 75 percent of the total growth of 2013, while most advanced economies are still with slow growth challenges, high unemployment, and very uncertain financial markets. Merging market growth will be helped by stronger external demand from advanced economies, but tighter financial conditions will dampen domestic demand growth. In China, growth is projected to remain at about 7½ percent in 2014 as the authorities seek to rein in credit and advance reforms while ensuring a gradual transition to a more balanced and sustainable growth path.

After seven years since the global financial crisis, global recovery is still fragile despite improved prospects, and significant downside risks—both old and new—remain. Recently, some new geopolitical risks have emerged. On old risks, those related to emerging market economies have increased with the changing external environment. Unexpectedly, rapid normalization of U.S. monetary policy or renewed bouts of high-risk aversion on the part of investors could result in further financial turmoil. This would lead to difficult adjustments in some emerging market economies, with a risk of contagion and broad-based financial stress, and thus lower growth.

Advanced Economies Fiscal Deficit

The average fiscal deficit for advanced economies is about seven percent of its GDP, almost two percent more than those of emerging markets, and it is likely this trend will continue for the next few years due to the high risk of fiscal sustainability. In our opinion, advanced economies should strive to balance their fiscal consolidation objectives and strengthen their economic growth. Figure 3.1 provides a real-time (as of June 10, 2014) overall listing of the external debt to GDP ratios of major economies in the world, both advanced and emerging.

As depicted in Figure 3.1, the financial crisis that began in late 2007, with its mix of liquidity crunch, decreased tax revenues, huge economic stimulus programs, recapitalizations of banks, and so on and so forth,

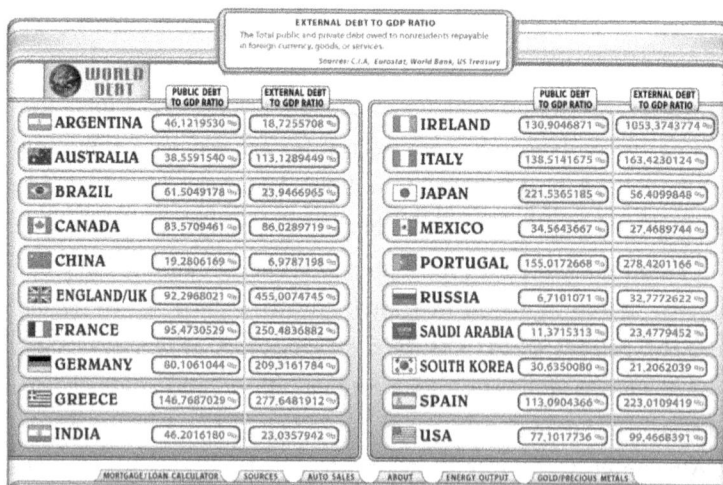

EXTERNAL DEBT TO GDP RATIO
The Total public and private debt owed to nonresidents repayable in foreign currency, goods, or services.
Sources: C.I.A., Eurostat, World Bank, US Treasury

WORLD DEBT	PUBLIC DEBT TO GDP RATIO	EXTERNAL DEBT TO GDP RATIO		PUBLIC DEBT TO GDP RATIO	EXTERNAL DEBT TO GDP RATIO
ARGENTINA	46.1219530 %	18.7255708 %	IRELAND	130.9046871 %	1053.3743774 %
AUSTRALIA	38.5591540 %	113.1289449 %	ITALY	138.5141675 %	163.4230124 %
BRAZIL	61.5049178 %	23.9466965 %	JAPAN	221.5365185 %	56.4099848 %
CANADA	83.5709461 %	86.0289719 %	MEXICO	34.5643667 %	27.4689744 %
CHINA	19.2806169 %	6.9787198 %	PORTUGAL	155.0172668 %	278.4201166 %
ENGLAND/UK	92.2968021 %	455.0074745 %	RUSSIA	6.7101071 %	32.7772622 %
FRANCE	95.4730529 %	250.4836882 %	SAUDI ARABIA	11.3715313 %	23.4779452 %
GERMANY	80.1061044 %	209.3161784 %	SOUTH KOREA	30.6350080 %	21.2062039 %
GREECE	146.7687029 %	277.6481912 %	SPAIN	113.0904366 %	223.0109419 %
INDIA	46.2016180 %	23.0357942 %	USA	77.1017736 %	99.4668391 %

MORTGAGE/LOAN CALCULATOR   SOURCES   AUTO SALES   ABOUT   ENERGY OUTPUT   GOLD/PRECIOUS METALS

Figure 3.1 World public and external debt to GDP ratio

Source: CIA, Eurostat, World Bank, and U.S. Treasury.

led to a dramatic increase in the public debt for most advanced economies. Public debt as a percent of GDP in OECD countries as a whole went from hovering around 70 percent throughout the 1990s to almost 110 percent in 2012. It is now projected to grow to 112.5 percent of GDP in 2014, possibly rising even higher in the following years. This trend is visible not only in countries with a history of debt problems, such as Japan, Italy, Belgium, and Greece, but also in countries where it was relatively low before the crisis, such as the United States, UK, France, Portugal, and Ireland.

Many analysts see this high level of debt as being unsustainable in many countries, with the eurozone in the center of this crisis. Indeed, throughout 2010, 2011, and even 2012, speculators were betting on defaults by Greece, and possibly Italy, Spain, and Portugal. Some countries are in a better position, like France and Germany. However, even here rating agencies are tweaking with credit ratings and threatening downgrades, bolstering fears that the EU could collapse under the weight of its members' debt. To respond to this emergency, governments across Europe have implemented painful austerity measures, which now are causing enormous political dissatisfaction, instability, and growing protests all over the euro currency union.

Conversely, some emerging markets are reaching the point where their economies are beginning to overheat, which generates inflationary challenges and making it harder to control capital flows. Such inflationary pressure in these markets is a sensitive issue, as food and basic products prices, which are included in the consumer price index (CPI) of many of these nations, such as India, Russia, and China, increase creating even more inflationary pressures. Notwithstanding, China has continued to register robust economic performance, creating many job opportunities, improving the standard of leaving of its people, and acting as an important generator of growth in the global economy.

As for advanced economies, the challenges these countries face, in particular the United States and the EU, are enormous. In early November 2013, the figures on growth, according to the U.S. federal government, continued to show signs of underlying economic weakness as EU's European Central Bank (ECB) unexpectedly cut interest rates to a record low, reflecting the threat of deflation.

According to a New York Times article,[1] written by Jack Ewing, out of Frankfurt, Germany, the U.S. economy would experience a 2.8 percent annualized growth for the third quarter, which turned out to be too optimistic, despite the fact that it was the fastest quarterly increase in output, well above the two percent economists expected. But nearly a full point of that jump was caused by a buildup in inventory, which can sap expansion. In reality, the annual rate of growth in consumer spending slowed sharply to 1.5 percent; the weakest quarterly increase in more than two years, while spending by the federal government fell 1.7 percent.

Olivier Blanchard, chief economist at the IMF, argued in October 2013 that advanced economies were strengthening, while emerging market economies were weakening.[2] Blanchard maintained that while fiscal risks in the United States, as worrisome as they are, should not lead investors to lose sight of the bigger picture, as the world economy has entered yet another transition, where advanced economies are slowly strengthening. At the same time, he contends emerging market economies have slowed down, more so than the IMF had predicted in July 2013.*

According to Blanchard, the growth should be around 1.2 percent in 2013 and 2.0 percent in 2014, while in emerging markets, it should be around 3.3 percent in 2013 and 3.1 percent in 2014, representing a slightly positive growth for advanced economies and slightly negative growth for emerging markets.

While the United States and the EU share many problems, it is clear the situation on much of the continent is much worse. Many economies in the EU are only now stabilizing after six quarters of renewed recession, and unemployment across the 17 nations that share the euro currency stands at roughly 12 percent. In especially hard-hit countries like Greece and Spain, the unemployment rate is more than twice that number. As of September 2013, the latest data on unemployment in the United States stood at 7.2 percent. Amid the United States' discouraging economic trends, in early November 2013 the consistently overly optimistic European Commission cut its growth forecast for 2014 to 1.1 percent from 1.2 percent.

Clearly, more than any other time in history, the United States and the EU's central banks are working together as much as possible trying

---

* Ibidem.

to prevent further deflation of their economies. The growth prospects in the United States were further compromised by a sudden drop in the eurozone inflation to an annual rate of 0.7 percent in October 2013, well below the ECB's official target of about two percent. The decline raised the threat of deflation and a sustained fall in prices that could destroy the confidence of consumers and the profits of companies, along with the jobs they provide.

While austerity rhetoric has taken root in both the United States and many European capitals, crimping fiscal policy, the course charted by central bankers in these two major advanced economies, in terms of monetary policy are beginning to go in different directions. Unlike the ECB, the U.S. Fed has moved aggressively to stimulate the economy, not only cutting short-term interest rates to near zero, but embarking on three rounds of asset purchases aimed at lowering borrowing rates and augmenting the growth rate.

Looking ahead, the picture for growth remains cloudy for most advanced economies, in particularly for the United States and the EU. We believe there are several economic and fiscal forces being played around the world today. The high indebtedness of advanced economies as a whole imposes major challenges for sustainable growth. In addition, emerging markets are still dependent on their exports to those nations, although these economies have begun diversifying their export market trading among each other with more frequency. The following is a brief overview of major global economic prospects for the main advanced economies and emerging markets, and how they are intertwined and impact one another.

The United States

The U.S. economy, despite being the largest economy in the world, has not recovered fully from the 2008 financial crisis and ensuing recession. The federal system of government, designed to reserve significant powers to the state and local levels, has been strained by the national government's rapid expansion. Spending at the national level rose to over 25 percent of GDP in 2010, and gross public debt surpassed 100 percent of GDP in 2011. Obamacare, a 2010 healthcare bill, greatly expanded the central government's regulatory role, and the Dodd–Frank financial overhaul bill roiled credit markets. In the same year, the election of a Republican

Party majority in the House of Representatives helped slow government spending down, but it divided the government, leaving economic policies in flux, which continued to endure well past the re-election of President Obama in 2012.

Economic freedom also is plummeting in the United States. According to the Heritage's 2013 Index of Economic freedom,[*,3] the United States has registered a loss of economic freedom for the fifth consecutive year, recording in 2013 its lowest Index score since 2000. Furthermore, the U.S. government has become increasingly more bloated, with trends toward cronyism that erodes the rule of law, thus stifling dynamic entrepreneurial growth. More than three years after the end of recession in June 2009, the United States continued to suffer from policy choices that led to the slowest recovery in 70 years. Overall, businesses remain in a holding pattern, except for some sectors, such as the military and biotech. Unemployment is close to 7.5 percent. Prospects for greater fiscal freedom are uncertain due to the scheduled expiration of previous cuts in income and payroll taxes, and the imposition of new taxes associated with the 2010 healthcare law.

As of fall 2013, Blanchard[†] contended that the private demand in the United States continued to be strong and that economic recovery should strengthen, assuming no fiscal accidents. We can't be sure of what he meant, but it seems logical that quantitative easing in the United States would need to continue for some time. Blanchard believes that while the immediate concern for the United States is with the government shutdown that happened in the fall of 2013, and making sure it doesn't recur, and the debt ceiling issue, the sequester policies implemented should lead to a fiscal consolidation into 2014, which is both too large and too arbitrary.

---

[*] The concept of *economic freedom*, or economic liberty, denotes the ability of members of a society to undertake economic direction and actions. This is a term used in economic and policy debates as well as a politico economic philosophy. One major approach to economic freedom comes from classical liberal and libertarian traditions emphasizing free markets, free trade, and private property under free enterprise, while another extends the welfare economics study of individual choice, with greater economic freedom coming from a "larger" set of possible choices.

[†] Ibidem.

Blanchard also argues that failure to lift the U.S. debt ceiling would be a game changer, which if prolonged would lead to an extreme fiscal consolidation, and surely derail the U.S. recovery. He continues, "The effects of any failure to repay the debt would be felt right away, leading to potentially major disruptions in financial markets, both in the United States and abroad. We [the IMF] see this as a tail risk, with low probability, but would have major consequences* if it were to happen." He recommended U.S. policymakers "make plans for exit from both quantitative easing and zero policy rates—although not time to implement them yet."[†]

At the time of this writing, in fall 2013, the debt ceiling discussion continues with the fiscal deal passed by Congress. The good news is that the government was able to reopen and attain the nearly $16.4 trillion dollar limit on borrowing. The bad news is that there is no actual debt ceiling right now, as the deal only temporarily suspended enforcement of it. For those intellectuals and economists who advocate the abolition of a debt ceiling all together, the current state of affairs is actually great news. That is the sky is the limit when it comes to U.S. government spending until February 7, 2014.

The fact that there is no dollar amount set for how much debt the government can accumulate through February 2014 is now tired-strategy, as it was first deployed earlier this year during previous fiscal battles in Congress, much to the dismay of many antigovernment waste groups.

Is it responsible governance for an advanced economy such as the United States, the largest economy in the world, to suspend a debt ceiling without a dollar amount? After all, common sense tells us that a real dollar figure in any budget, for a responsible individual or corporation, is a constant reminder of where we are in our personal or corporate finances. A dollar figure in a government's budget portrays how much it can spend, and the overall health of the country's finances.

It seems that a dollar figure in the United States federal budget may not be a good idea, especially when the country has credit agencies, such as Moody, Fitch, and Standards and Poor's (S&P) (although there may never be another downgrade of the U.S. economy by these agencies since

---

* Ibidem.
† Ibidem.

the U.S. government sued S&P for its downgrade), watching the United States and suggesting to taxpayers, Congress, and foreign investors that the United States may be broke.

In our research for this book, we spoke with many business executives from multinational companies, academic researchers, and professionals from around the world. Most of the professionals and executives we spoke to wondered aloud if the fiscal strategies now in place are designed to hide the true state of U.S. debt from its taxpayers, large foreign investors, and creditors on which the country depend. So, if we were to assume that there is some veracity in the aforementioned IMF assertions, it must be taken with a grain of salt. After all, we should not expect the IMF, so dependent on U.S. political support and funds, to be wholly unbiased.

Such strategies and polices undermine any informed investor, those capable of seeing through smokescreens. Any foreign investor and nation buying U.S. treasury bills will recognize a bad deal when they see it. Once these investors realize these Treasury bills are the equivalent of junk, regardless of the official rating, the buying will dry up and disastrous consequences will ensue in the financial markets and the U.S. economy as a whole.

As a disclaimer, the authors of this book do not claim to be economists. The proposition of this book to be written by noneconomists was by design. We are researchers and observers of what the data and the global trading dynamics tell us, especially between advanced economies and emerging markets. But it doesn't help to have a different opinion about the U.S economy, a less sanguine view. When the conservative Heritage Foundation[4] criticizes Washington's federal budget handling as a "smokescreen," alleging that the suspension of the debt ceiling is becoming increasingly less transparent to the American people, and that the U.S. government spending exceeds federal revenues by more than one trillion dollars, it is difficult not to have a gloomy outlook.

As shown in Figure 3.2, since 1973 (actually since 1965 but not showing in this graph), spending has been rising steadily. According to the U.S. Congressional Budget Office, the federal revenue and expenditure lines rarely intertwine. In the 40-year span from 1973 to 2013, spending exceeded income except from 1998 to 2002. The federal government borrows money to make up the difference between income and spending. Federal policymakers must struggle with the question of how high the federal debt should go. While federal revenues are recovering from the

Total revenues and outlays
(Percentage of gross product)

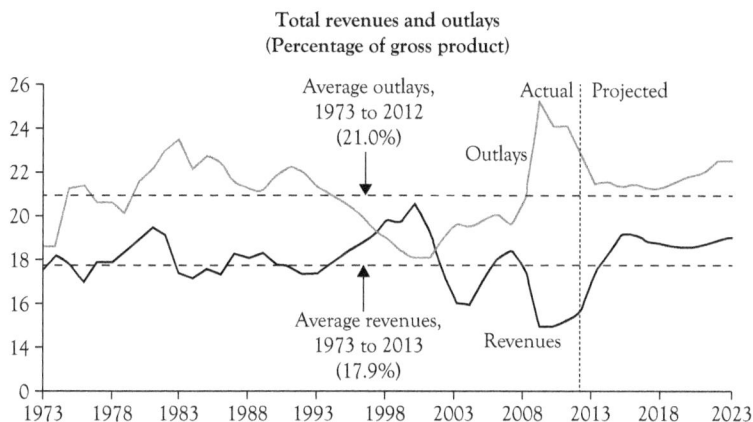

Figure 3.2 Federal spending exceeds federal revenue by more than $1 Trillion

Source: U.S. Office of Management and Budget.

recent recession, spending is growing sharply, resulting in four consecutive years of deficits exceeding one trillion.

Nonetheless, the U.S. Congress is still ignoring the proverbial elephant in the room, no matter how big and wide it gets as days go by, only so they can avoid debate on the specific dollar amount increase on the debt limit, thus making their political vote much easier to cast. It is much easier to vote on *when* we'll deal with a trillion dollar problem than to actually deal with the problem.

Huge swaths of the global financial system, including in advanced and emerging economies, is structured around the understanding that U.S. Treasuries are the safest asset in the world. What would happen if that assumption were ever called into question? We believe global financial havoc would ensue, which is precisely why Moody's thinks that a default on U.S. debt is unlikely, even if we smash into the debt ceiling.

Furthermore, if the U.S. Treasury wants to conserve enough cash to keep servicing the debt, then it will have to miss or delay several other important payments in the near future. If the U.S. Treasury pays the required $6 billion dollar interest payment by the end of October 2013, and another $29 billion dollars in interest payment by November 15, 2013, the United States may have no choice but to delay social security checks, Medicare payments, or military pay unless it borrows more from China, or simply print more money.

Restoring the United States to a place among the world's *free* economies will require significant policy reforms, particularly in reducing the size of government, overhauling the tax system, transforming costly entitlement programs, and streamlining regulations. Paraphrasing Mark Twain: history may not repeat itself and only rhymes. We do believe wholeheartedly in Ayn Rand's assertion[5] that every one of us builds our own world in our own image. We have the power to choose, but no power to escape the necessity of choice.

Japan

After 55 years of Liberal Democratic Party rule, the Democratic Party of Japan captured both houses of parliament in 2009 and installed Yukio Hatoyama as prime minister. Hatoyama resigned abruptly in June 2010 and was succeeded by Finance Minister Naoto Kan, who was replaced in September 2011 by Yoshihiko Noda. The March 2011 earthquake and tsunami further strained the beleaguered economy, which has been struggling for nearly two decades with slow growth and stagnation. Prime Minister Noda strived to include Japan in the TPP to stimulate the economy but faced strong resistance at home. Successive prime ministers have been unable or unwilling to implement necessary fiscal reforms. As a result of this long and persistent economic crisis, Japan's economy is still about the same size as it was in 1992. In essence, Japan has lost more than two decades of growth.[6] The 2008 global financial crisis and the 2011 Great East Japan Earthquake only aggravated the situation, imposing two severe and consecutive shocks to the Japanese economy. The earthquake alone, the worst disaster in Japan's postwar history, killed nearly 20,000 people and caused enormous physical damage.

According to the OECD,[7] prior to the global economic and financial crisis, as shown in Figure 3.3, Japan's initial strong recovery from the earthquake and tsunami stalled in mid-2012, leaving output 2.5 percent below the peak recorded in 2008. The earthquake and tsunami only compounded Japan's distressed economy. The country has experienced three recessions in less than five years.

Consequently, the major challenge for Japan's economy is to find a way to achieve sustained growth and fiscal sustainability following these two major disasters; the country suffered a 0.7 percent loss in real GDP in 2008 followed by a severe 5.2 percent loss in 2009. Exports from Japan also

Real GDP levels in an index with the first quarter of 2007 set at 100

Index

Index

106

104

102

100

98

96

94

92

— Japan
— OECD
--- USA
..... Euro area

106

104

102

100

98

96

94

92

2007   2008   2009   2010   2011   2012

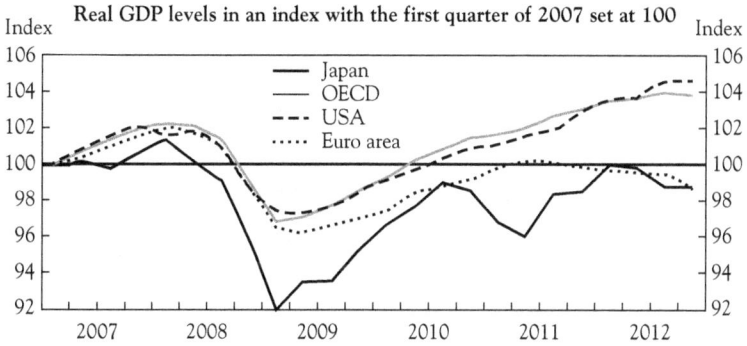

Figure 3.3 Japan has faced two major economic shocks since 2008

Source: OECD Economic Outlook Database.

shrunk from $746.5 billion dollars to $545.3 billion dollars from 2008 to 2009, a 27 percent reduction.* Japan is as handcuffed by its own rigidities as any other country. What is worrisome is that while some export-oriented industries have remained competitive, the Japanese domestic economy appears to be held hostage by bureaucracy, tradition, and overregulation.

Other countries would do well to take note of this conundrum as the same concerns Japanese businesses face certainly would affect businesses globally. It is the authors' suggestion that both advanced and emerging economies should take on these challenges, even the stalwart ones of old Europe: Spain, Italy, and France. These all tend to be myopic toward a focus on domestic consumption instead of savings and investments. Often, insufficient attention is given to the unattractive, frequently politically toxic load of smaller policy challenges that can be critical to restarting a faltering economy. For the purpose of reference, in 2011, global real GDP growth was up a 3.9 percent,[8] as depicted in Figure 3.4, while Japan had fallen below global growth at −0.7 percent.

Furthermore, Japan's public debt ratio, as shown in Figure 3.5 has risen steadily for two decades, exceeding 200 percent of GDP. Therefore, the country must promote strong and protracted consolidation to mitigate fiscal sustainability. This is by far Japan's major policy challenge; as such policy will decelerate nominal GDP growth, making fiscal adjustments still more difficult. Ending deflation and boosting Japan's growth

---

* Ibidem.

GDP - real growth rate (%)

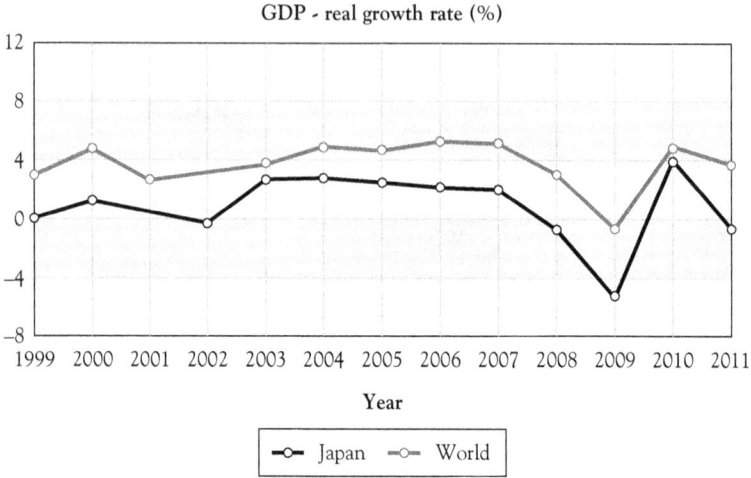

Figure 3.4 Japan's economy has fallen below global growth

Gross public debt

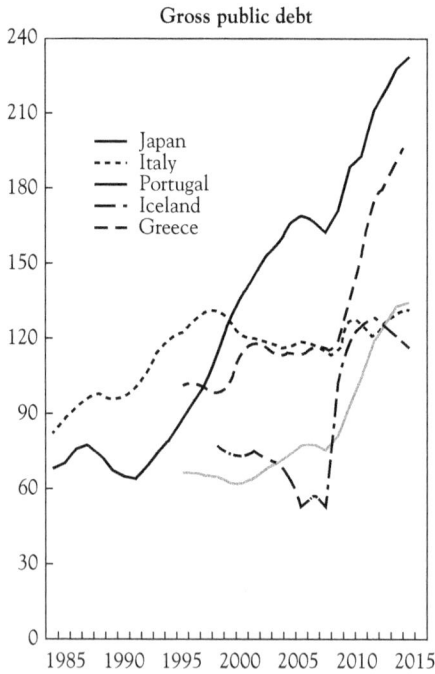

Figure 3.5 Japan's gross public debt as percentage of the GDP

Source: OECD Economic Outlook, No 92, and revised OECD estimates and projections for Japan for 2012–14.

potential is imperative in addressing the fiscal predicament in which it finds itself. Consequently, Japan's new government's determination to revitalize the economy through a three-leg strategy combining bold monetary policy, flexible fiscal policy, and a growth strategy is not only necessary, but admirable.

One immediate way the country is responding to the crisis, according to Kathy Matsui,[9] chief Japan equity strategist for Global Investment Research with Goldman Sachs, is by Japanese companies buying companies overseas, more so than we have seen to date. Whether the recovery in Japan continues, it can only be sustained by Abenomics* policies in meeting two major challenges. The first, reflected in the debate about an increase in the consumption tax, is the right pace of fiscal consolidation as it should not be either too slow and compromise credibility, or too fast and stymie growth. The second is a credible set of structural reforms to transform a cyclical recovery into sustained growth.

Hopefully the Tokyo stock market will continue to rally. The Japanese yen and its stock market have benefited from Abenomics expansionary policies. Having lost as much as 18 percent by mid-May 2013, the yen currently is down around 12 percent on the year, which is a windfall for a currency-sensitive exporter country like Japan. In the fall of 2012, the economy surged 65 percent, while in the second quarter of 2013, the economy expanded by 3.8 percent, faster than any other advanced economy. Prices are edging upward, which is a good thing for Japan's fight on deflation. Yet, the disposition in Tokyo among businessmen and economists remains perilously balanced between enthusiasm for the monetary and fiscal stimulus unleashed by Abenomics, and concern that promised structural reforms might not be implemented.

The European Union

As of fall 2013, the EU has shown some signs of recovery. This is not due, however, to major policy changes, as in Japan, but partly to a change in mood, which could be a self-fulfilling prophecy. Southern periphery

---

* The term *Abenomics* is a portmanteau of "Abe" and "economics," which refers to the economic policies advocated by Shinzō Abe, the current Prime Minister of Japan.

countries, such as Spain, Greece, Italy, and Portugal, still struggle as defi-
nite progress on competitiveness and exports are not yet strong enough to
offset depressed internal demand. Hence, there is still much uncertainty
in the EU, the largest economy in the world as a bloc. Bank balance
sheets remain an issue, but should be reduced according to the promised *asset quality review* recommended by European Banking Authority
(EBA). Such close scrutiny of EU's banks may turn up unexpected short-
falls though. Like Japan, larger structural reforms are urgently needed to
increase the anemic potential growth rates of the EU.

The Olive Growers Uncertain Faith and the Euro

The debt crisis continues to overwhelm Europe, and the prospects for
countries most entrenched in debt, including Portugal, Italy, Greece,
Spain, and Ireland, are dismal. Worse, regardless of whether these countries voluntarily leave or are coerced to leave, it is conceivable that Germany may opt to go solo. The not-so-popular George Soros argues that
the euro crisis is far worse than earlier estimations, suggesting that it could
eventually end up dissolving the EU.

In a Berlin speech in late April 2012, Soros indicated that the EU
crisis casts a shadow on the global economy, a consequence of its own
political evolution. He argues that the Maastricht Treaty,*,† which led to
the creation of the euro, and created what was commonly referred to as
the pillar structure of the European Union, was fundamentally flawed, as
it established a monetary union without a political one. In essence, the
euro was launched without any real democratic consultation or approval,
intended by world leaders as political glue in the march toward pan-Eu-
ropean sovereignty.

---

* The Maastricht Treaty (formally, the Treaty on European Union or TEU)
was signed on 7 February 1992 by the members of the European Community
in Maastricht, Netherlands. On 9–10 December 1991, the same city hosted
the European Council which drafted the treaty. Upon its entry into force on
1 November 1993 during the Delors Commission, it created the European
Union and led to the creation of the single European currency, the euro.
† "1990–1999." The history of the European Union—1990–1999. Europa. Last
accessed on 09/11/2011.

Whereas global analysts and the mainstream media seem to overlook much of this threat to the world's second largest reserve currency, the more immediate concern is the possibility that Germany will abdicate from the EU, causing the euro to plummet, which could subsequently trigger a major international monetary crisis. The EU may survive with a few less olive growers such as Portugal and Greece, but certainly not without the solid backing of Germany.

While the world watches with hopeful expectations for the first time in history, the synchronicity of the central banks of Europe, UK, China, India, Japan, and the United States" printing fresh money and increasing the base supplies of their respective countries, we tend to forget important historic facts about Germany and the eurozone. Namely, Germany was never sanguine about the euro from the onset. In fact, most Europeans were not. We view it more as a quid pro quo case, whereby Germans accepted the euro in exchange for France's support of Germany's post-Cold War reunification. Trading the Deutsche mark for the euro, in and of itself, did not equate logically.

EU's dire situation provides Germany with an opportunity to augment its political influence in the region, and a return on its investment of the euro, by way of financial rescue packages to olive growers. However, if such efforts fail, as is likely the case, Germany will have no compelling reason to remain with the EU, since Europeans are already becoming resentful of Germany and the EU. History has shown us time and again that austerity breed's political disgust, particularly when imposed by outside powers. A pro-German government in Holland has already fallen in local elections, and President Sarkozy lost ground in his re-election campaign, eventually losing the elections, precisely due to his perceived support of German policy. Then there are the German people who resist the idea of seeing their hard-earned money squandered on people who refuse to tighten their belts.

The central bank's printing of money and Germany's financial packages are not ameliorating the situation. On the contrary, the olive growers are not alone. Many other countries are already in recession, including Slovenia, Italy, the Czech Republic, Ireland, Denmark, Netherlands, Belgium, and the UK. Whether the euro endures, Europe and especially the olive growing countries are facing a long period of economic stagnation. We witnessed Latin American countries suffer a similar fate in the early 80s, and Japan, which has been in stagnation for almost a quarter century. While they have survived, the eurozone situation is graver, as the EU is not a single country but rather a union of many; the lingering deflationary debt trap threatens to destroy a still nascent political union.

We believe that only when a friendlier monetary policy and a milder fiscal austerity is proposed will the euro remain strong. This will weaken the eurozone's exports' competitiveness, and drag the recession to even lower levels, which in turn will force more eurozone countries to restructure their debts and may cause some to ultimately exit the euro.

EU's Economic Prospects

The Economist magazine expects GDP will stagnate across the 28 largest economies within the EU in 2013, after falling by 0.5 percent in 2012, and expand by 1.4 percent in 2014. This is according to forecasts from the European Commission in early November 2013, as this chapter was written. Across the 17 largest countries in the EU, however, a weak recovery has begun, following a double-dip recession lasting 18 months. For 2013, GDP in the EU will fall by 0.4 percent, after falling by 0.6 percent in 2012. In 2014, GDP is expected to rise by 1.1 percent. Figure 3.6 provides information on GDP growth by country for those in the EU euro area, those pegged to the euro, and those countries floating their currency as of the first quarter of 2013.

As was the case in 2013, growth in 2014 will be strongest (4.1 percent) in Latvia, which is poised to join the euro area in January. Indeed the three Baltic countries, including Lithuania outside the eurozone and Estonia already in it, will be the three fastest-growing economies in the EU. But the main impetus behind the euro area's recovery will be a combination of German growth of 1.7 percent coupled with a more modest return to growth in Italy and Spain, the region's third and fourth biggest economies. Outside the eurozone, Sweden and Britain are expected to do well in 2014, with growth of 2.8 percent and 2.2 percent, respectively.

The worse performers for 2014 are two countries also in the eurozone. Both Cyprus and Slovenia will experience a decrease on GDP. Cyprus' distresses will continue, with a further contraction, of 3.9 percent, while

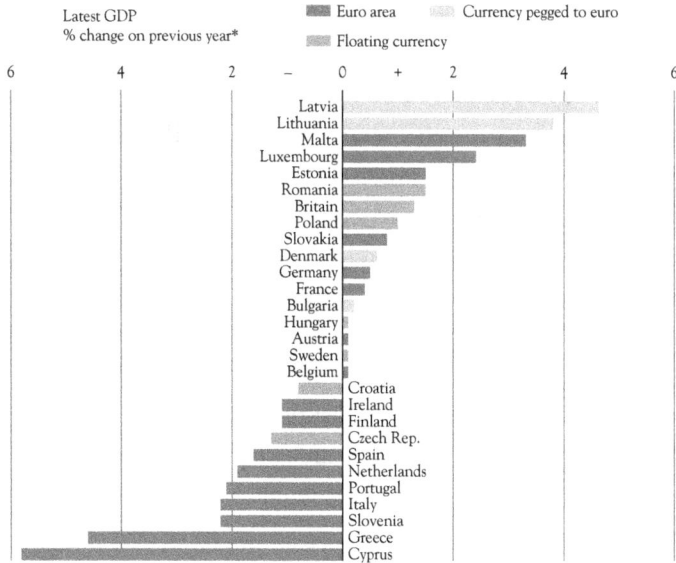

Figure 3.6 GDP growth across the EU countries

Source: Eurostat.

Slovenia's GDP also will slide again, by 1 percent. Nonetheless, such prospects should be considered positive. GDP is expected to fall in eight countries in the eurozone and ten in the EU. Lastly, this minor recovery in 2014 should not bring much joy for the jobless, as unemployment in the eurozone is expected to stay at 12.2 percent in 2014. This statistic is much higher with olive grower countries; Spain is registering 32 percent youth unemployment as of fall 2014.

We believe the euro area has the potential to take advantage of the global opportunities, especially emerging markets. The euro area is more open to trade than many other advanced economies. The EU's exports and imports of goods and services account for around one fifth of GDP, more than in the United States or Japan. The EU has been open to the idea of emerging markets. Its trade relations with emerging markets such as Asia, Turkey, and Russia, for instance, as well as with central and eastern European countries, have strengthened noticeably over the past decade. Taken together, the share of emerging markets in the euro area trade has grown from about 33 percent, when the euro was introduced in 1999, to more than 40 percent as of 2013.[10]

One aspect less well known about the eurozone is that it is financially very flexible and open. The international balance sheet of the eurozone, its assets and liabilities vis-à-vis nonresidents account, is over 120 percent and 130 percent of euro area GDP, respectively. This is more than in many other advanced economies such as the United States, where the corresponding figures are 90 percent and 110 percent of GDP. In addition, according to Trading Economics,[11] the EU is becoming increasingly open. Since the euro was created, the size of the eurozone area's external assets and liabilities has grown by about 40 percent. Hence, if we were to focus on emerging markets alone, one of the most interesting developments in recent years is the fact that the eurozone has become an attractive destination for FDI from the largest of these economies. For instance, during 1999 to 2005, the amount of FDI from Brazil, Russia, India, and China in the eurozone tripled, to about €12 billion euros ($16.2 billion).

Emerging Markets

The long-term fundamentals for emerging market growth, we believe, are directly linked to the potential for emerging market companies to tap into the favorable long-term economic growth prospects for all the emerging economies. As pointed out in earlier chapters, those growth prospects are based on two main factors: positive demographic trends (with some exceptions) and balance sheets that are not reliant on and burdened by debt, as seen across advanced economies. Combined, these are potent and sustainable benefits for emerging markets.

The rising population numbers that many emerging nations are experiencing help to ensure that aggregate demand will grow faster while the strong and underleveraged balance sheets–of both consumers and sovereigns–help to assure investors that the pace of investments and consumption can be kept in balance. This is in contrast to the deleveraging process—both at the government and consumer level—that will take years to run its course in many developed markets. Such deleveraging will continue to exert strong deflationary pressures on these developed economies. While there is a great deal of uncertainty as to how developed-market central banks will counter these pressures, any expansion of global liquidity should favor assets with better growth prospects, such as the ones found in emerging market economies.

We believe, however, that emerging markets need to exercise some caution (driven by the prospects for liquidity withdrawal), should the U.S Federal reserve and the ECB, as well as other advanced economies' central banks, begin to shutter their quantitative easing programs. Relatedly, we see signs that currency and interest rates in many emerging markets need to adjust to more sustainable equilibriums. For instance, in the BRICS bloc, currencies need to depreciate and real interest rates need to rise. While this may be tough to enact, it is necessitated by the deterioration of the aggregate current account balance of the emerging market universe since 2007, which has been caused by the weak demand from advanced economies, weakening commodity prices, and the *stimulating* domestic demand policies that have prevailed in many emerging markets since the global financial crisis.

Emerging markets will need to weather financial market turbulence and maintain high medium-term growth. The appropriate policy measures will differ across these economies. However, many of them have some policy priorities in common:

- First, policymakers should allow exchange rates to respond to changing fundamentals and facilitate external adjustment. Where international reserves are adequate, foreign exchange interventions can be used to smooth volatility and avoid financial disruption.
- Second, in economies in which inflation is still relatively high or the risks that recent currency depreciation could feed into underlying inflation are high, further monetary policy tightening may be necessary. If policy credibility is a problem, strengthening the transparency and consistency of policy frameworks may be necessary for tightening to be effective.
- Third, on the fiscal front, policymakers must lower budget deficits, although the urgency for action varies across economies. Early steps are required if public debt is already elevated and the associated refinancing needs are a source of vulnerability.

- Fourth, many economies need a new round of structural reforms that include investment in public infrastructure, removal of barriers to entry in product and services markets, and in China, rebalancing growth away from investment toward consumption.

A correction already has started as many emerging market currencies have been depreciating against the U.S. dollar and the euro for nearly a year. These downward trends have been distinctly unfavorable since the rebound at the end of the crisis. We also are starting to see some upward ticks in interest rates in certain countries. As part of this adjustment, there is a possibility that we will see lower economic growth, which could be negative for earnings-growth expectations. The market has already started to discount this notion as seen through the lower valuations of emerging versus advanced economies.

The causes for such trends vary in opinion. There is a belief that emerging markets may be in a cyclical slowdown. Another belief is that emerging markets are now experiencing a decrease in growth potential. We believe, based on our own research that both are true. Extraordinarily favorable world conditions, be it strong commodity prices or global financial conditions, led to higher potential growth in the 2000s, with, in a number of countries, a cyclical component on top. As commodity prices began to stabilize and financial conditions tightened, potential growth is lowered and, in some cases, compounded by a sharp cyclical adjustment. Faced with these conditions, governments in emerging markets are now faced with two challenges: adjust to lower potential growth, and, where needed, deal with the cyclical adjustment.

Considering a potential slow down on these economies, at least when compared to the 2000 rates, structural reforms not only will be necessary, but urgent. Such structural reforms may include rebalancing toward consumption in China, or removing barriers to investment in India or Brazil. Regarding cyclical adjustments, the typical standard advice from macroeconomics applies, such as the consolidation of debt in countries with large fiscal deficits. Countries with inflation running persistently above government targets, such as in Vietnam and Indonesia, a tighter and, even more importantly, more credible monetary policy framework must be implemented.

Frontier markets and other low-income countries must avoid a buildup of external and public debt. Many of these countries have succeeded in maintaining strong growth, partly reflecting better macroeconomic policies, but their external environment has also been changing. Foreign direct investment has started to moderate with declining commodity prices, and commodity-related budget revenues and foreign exchange earnings are at risk. Timely policy adjustments will be important to avoid a buildup in external debt and public debt.

When assessing the prospects for advanced economies, the architecture of the financial system is still evolving, and its future shape and soundness are still unclear. Unemployment remains too high, which will continue to be a major challenge for several years to come. As for emerging markets, and the implications of its rise in the world economy, the impact is multifaceted, and already is being felt around the globe. It encompasses two areas of immediate concern for central bankers in those countries and around the world, namely global inflation and global capital flows.

The Impact of Emerging Markets Rise on the Global Economy

The integration into the global economy of a massive pool of low-cost, skilled workers from emerging markets has tended to exert downward pressure on import prices of manufactured goods and wages in advanced economies.[12] Emerging markets have significantly contributed to the increase of the labor force and the reduction of labor costs around the world. The available labor force in the global economy has actually doubled from 1.5 to 3 billion, mainly as a reflection of the opening up of China, India, and Russia's economies.[13] The price of a wide range of manufactured goods has declined over the years. Furthermore, through numerous channels, this process of wage restrains and reduced inflationary pressure in the manufacturing sector also has affected wage dynamics and distribution in the services sector, mainly due to outsourcing. Consequently, these effects have contributed to the dampening of inflationary pressures.

Conversely, there are opposing dynamics to be considered between advanced economies and emerging markets. Some resources, such as energy and food, have become relatively scarce over time due to the increased demand from emerging economies, such as China and India.

We believe this may have been a source of increased inflationary pressure over the past few years, although we acknowledge that it is difficult to make an exact assessment of this contribution, since commodity prices also are affected by supply conditions and geopolitical factors. Nonetheless, according to Pain, Koske, and Sollie's study,[14] the rapid growth in emerging countries and their increasing share in world trade and GDP may have contributed to an increase in oil prices by as much as 40 percent, and real metal prices by as much as 10 percent in the first five years of the new millennium.

All in all, it is difficult to measure accurately the total impact of emerging markets on inflation. For instance, the IMF has estimated that globalization, through its direct effects on nonoil import prices, has reduced inflation on average by 0.25 percent per year in advanced economies.[15] The overall impact, however, is more difficult to estimate and extricate from other factors that could reduce inflation. For example, the increase in productivity growth and the stronger credibility of monetary policy are two impending factors.

A New Form of Capitalism

Recently, Dr. Goncalves returned from China, and during his return flight, he came to the realization that although he teaches on the subject of China in his international business program at Nichols College, he had missed the point when it came to that country's profile. He kept thinking about how Taipei, a democracy in Taiwan, with all of its tall gray buildings seemed more like a communist country than China. In contrast, Hong Kong's Time Square, the World Trade Centre, Causeway Bay, and its SOHO seemed more like Manhattan on steroids. Despite the plethora of books and articles he's read on the subject, he came to realize that Chinese communism today isn't anything like his antiquated vision of it, which was formed by living in the United States and shaped by the Soviet Union (now Russia).

The communism he witnessed in Hong Kong and Macau, although we must note these two countries are China's Special Administration Regions (SARs), are true examples of capitalism at its core. In contrast to the West and most advanced economies today, unemployment rates in

Hong Kong and Macau are only four and two percent respectively. Hong Kong hosts the most skyscrapers in the world, with New York City a distant second, with only half the amount. Hong Kong also holds the most Rolls Royce's in the world. Macau's per capita income is $68 thousand, in contrast to $48 thousand in the United States.

What impacted him the most during his 21 days there was the optimism of it's people. This is in contrast to the cynicism heard constantly in the West, where people seem to have lost their excitement about the future. There, young and old, people yearn and strive for more than what they have. He agrees with Goldman Sachs' Jim O'Neill, who coined the "BRIC countries" back in 2000, in his assertion that "China is the greatest story of our generation."[16] China's general macroeconomics is very promising. It scores well for its stable inflation, external financial position, government debt, investment levels, and openness to foreign trade. At the microlevel it falls just below average on corruption and use of technology. But, the latter is changing rapidly.

There simply is no overstating China's importance to us all, particularly the West, notwithstanding the 1.3 billion Chinese. Like it or not, we must realize that the entire planet, all 6.5 billion, is and must be invested in China's success. Doubts? In 1995, China's economy was worth roughly $500 billion. In just 16 years it has grown more than tenfold. By 2001, its GDP was $1.5 trillion, at the time it was smaller than the United Kingdom and France. Today, China is the second largest economy in the world.

Undeniably, it will be a hard road for China to maintain its consistent 9 to 10 percent annual growth moving forward. Their growth rates will most certainly decelerate. The question is by how much and how smoothly. In March 2014, the government announced a 7.5 percent growth target for its thirteenth five-year plan. This is best for its economy and people so that policy makers can better focus on the quality of the growth, instead of sheer quantity. After all, no country can sustain growth by building ghost cities as China has been doing. The good news is that China does not have to maintain the 10 percent GDP growth pace in order to continue to grow and actually surpass the United States to become the largest economy in the world. For now, China is still only about one third of the U.S. economy (in comparable dollar terms).

It appears that China's Communist Party, with 80 million members, is not just the world's largest political party but also its biggest chamber of commerce. That can be worrisome, as China's influence and impact on all advanced and emerging markets around the world looms large. The eurozone crises have many of us in the United States concerned. As it deteriorates, it will impact Wall Street and the United States economy. However, anything that happens in China is far more important and impactful to the fate of the world economy than the eurozone crises.

China's Challenges

As Brazil, Russia, India, and China, the BRIC countries, advance full-steam ahead. Jim O'Neil's decade-old prediction for this group of only four countries remains prescient. BRIC is growing an economy that will surpass the combined size of the great G-8 economies by 2035.* Very little is said, however, about China's shattering stories of the hordes of small business owners committing suicide, leaving China, or flat out emigrating to the West. It makes me wonder how much vested interest Goldman Sachs has in such predictions.

Don't get us wrong. We are avid proponents of the rise and formidable influence the BRIC countries are having on the global economy. In Dr. Goncalves' Advanced Economies and Emerging Market classes, students are exposed to detailed characteristics of the engine propelling the BRICs, its impact on the G-8, and how to position themselves professionally to capitalize on it. But, we cannot ignore the public outcry of Chinese entrepreneurs facing the deterioration of business conditions in that country.

The somewhat positive step taken by the People's Bank of China (PBOC) in December 2012, to alleviate China's alleged liquidity crisis, should cause us to reassess the sustainability of its economy at current rates. China is far from a liquidity crisis, however, possessing an M2[†] that

---

* Ibidem, pg. 201.

[†] A category within the money supply that includes M1 in addition to all time-related deposits, savings deposits, and noninstitutional money-market funds. M2 is a broader classification of money than M1. Economists use M2 when looking to quantify the amount of money in circulation and trying to explain different economic monetary conditions. Source: Investopedia,

has surpassed the United States, reaching nearly $11.55 trillion. This was due, in part, by reducing the reserve requirement ratio*, (RRR), to 21 percent from its record high of 21.5 percent.

It is not clear to us whether China is on a sustainable economic path, at least until it slows down its equity investments and begins to pay more attention to and empower its middle class. The Chinese people won't be willing to spend if they don't have a decent health or retirement system, which impels them to save, on average, 30 percent of their income. China's obsession with extreme growth, sustained now for over a decade, has become the huge white elephant for global markets. Unless the Chinese government begins to deal diligently with this issue, it may not be able to prevent an epic hard landing of its economy.

Much like Western economies, China blames the tightening of monetary policy as the feeder of its ever-growing white elephant. Again, much like the West, it looks more like a systemic issue, since its main markets, the United States and Europe, are both battling a probable imminent double recession, which is squeezing their buying power. In addition, ahead of the West, inflation is rising. Wage inflation is causing the hungry elephant to erode China's main competitive advantage in the manufacturing industry. The tightening of monetary policy is anathema to this, but the transformative systemic change in the Chinese economy isn't. Just look at the Purchasing Manager Index[†] (PMI), which dropped to 49 in December, much lower than market expectations, to realize that the manufacturing sector is bleeding. In early 2013 the PMI climbed to 53, but manufacturing goods in China have been declining. As depicted in Figure 3.7, in October 2013, China's PMI fell to 52.6, and even further, to 50.2 in February 2014.

---

* The portion (expressed as a percent) of depositors' balances banks must have on hand as cash. This is a requirement determined by the country's central bank, which in the United States is the Federal Reserve. The reserve ratio affects the money supply in a country. This is also referred to as the "cash reserve ratio" (CRR).
[†] A monthly index of manufacturing, considered one of the most reliable leading indicators available to assess the near-term direction of an economy. An index reading above 50 percent indicates that the manufacturing sector is generally expanding, while a reading below 50 percent indicates contraction. The further the index is away from 50 percent, the greater the rate of change.

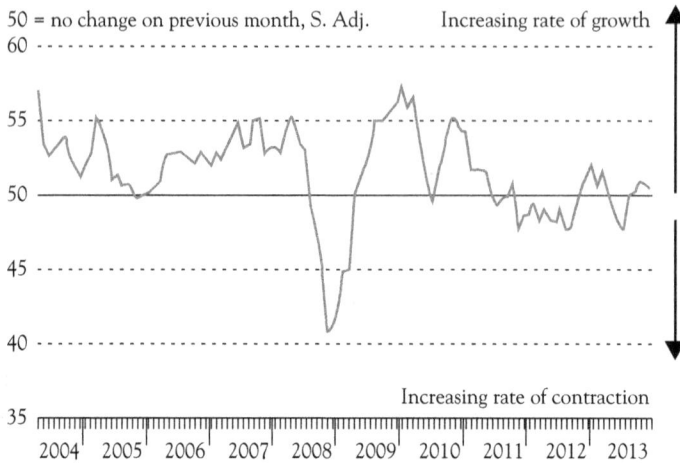

Figure 3.7 China manufacturing PMI as of December 2013[17]

Source: Markit Economics, HSBC1.

Such declines in PMI produce a ripple effect of stocks piling up, thereby driving up the cost of doing business. So much so that it has become cheaper for China to transfer its manufacturing to the United States, primarily to South Carolina. Certainly, labor costs, even in the south of the United States, are higher than in China. But the cost of energy is a lot cheaper, as is the cost of real estate, infrastructure, and shipping across the Pacific.

What makes China's white elephant so pale is that small and medium businesses (SMBs), the driving force of China's manufacturing, do not have easy access to credit. China's four major banks, Bank of China, the China Construction Bank, the Industrial and Commercial Bank of China, and the Agricultural Bank of China, control more than 70 percent of China's banking market. These are state-owned banks which favor state-owned companies, and, rarely, some fortunate private corporations. This resource misallocation is feeding the pallid pachyderm at the expense of SMBs, left with their only option of costly business financing.

We do not profess to be economists, but looking at the sheer size of China's white elephant, it is clear to us that monetary policy alone cannot fix the systemic insufficiencies of China's economy. As long as the economy remains vastly dependent on the United States and European consumerism, countries currently dealing with their own herd of white elephants, and unable to consume as before, China's exports will remain massively strained. Consequently, the country is being burdened with a severe excess capacity problem, pushing down the marginal returns of investment and GDP, while fostering an uptick of inflation, unemployment, and possibly more bubbles.

As the United States and Europe deal with their own economic crisis, they are being forced to place their deficit-fueled consumption economies on a stringent diet. To deal with their own white elephant they will have to shop and consume less, to give room for increasing saving rates which is chronically low at the moment, and higher productivity. Such an unavoidable consumer diet could be disastrous for China, as data from the Economist Intelligence Unit and the U.S. Department of Commerce's (DOC) Bureau of Economic Analysis suggests that China will remain dependent on an export-led economy until at least late 2030. If true, China must find new markets and reduce its dependence on the West's economies.

Could the BRIC countries be the ace under China's sleeves? After all, as O'Neil predicted, in the next two decades these four countries will account for half of the population of the entire world (i.e., huge middle-class), and their economies will be larger than the G-7 countries combined. Europe today has 35 cities with a population over one million, but by 2030, India alone will have 68 cities with over one million and China will have over one billion consumers living in cities. This staggering fact alone could mark the slow death of China's white elephant, by letting go of its dependence on the West, and the return of a progressive flame-throwing dragon, ready to sizzle its middle-class economy and the BRIC's with sales aplenty of manufactured goods.

The question remains which will have more weight: the shortsighted state-capitalist elephant or the farsighted free-market driven dragon?

Brazil: An Economy of Extremes

Dr. Goncalves recently returned from Brazil, and while observing the hustle and bustle of Rio's international airport, busier than ever, it dawned on him that Brazil has much to be proud of. He is Brazilian, and therefore, admits to being a tad biased, but the fact remains that a decade of accelerated growth and progressive social policies have brought the country prosperity that is ever more widely shared. The unemployment rate as of September 2013 was 5.4 percent, up from 5.30 percent in August of 2013.* Credit is flourishing, however, particularly to the swelling number of people who have moved out of poverty status and into the ranks of the middle class. Income inequality, though still high, has fallen sharply.

For most Brazilians life has never been as hopeful, and to some extent we see plenty of paradigm shifts. Women's salaries are growing twice as fast as those of men, even though they only occupy a mere 21.4 percent of executive positions and despite the fact they hold most of the doctoral degrees in the country (51.5 percent) and dominate the area of research (58.6 percent). Women also own more companies in the Latin American region (11 percent) than any other emerging country. The new shifts in the Brazilian economy also benefit the black communities, which have seen their salaries increase four times faster than their white counterparts, bringing the population of the middle class blacks from 39.3 percent to 50.9 percent. According to research conducted by the Federal University of Rio de Janeiro, of 20.6 million people who entered the workplace, only 7.7 million were white. Overall, the country is enjoying the boom brought by commodities, in particular oil and gas, despite the global economic slowdown. Are advanced economies entrepreneurs taking advantage of this?

If not, they should, but with a caveat. We believe what worked for the Brazilian economy ten even twenty years ago, such as a focus on commodities, low labor costs, and excessive focus on exports, won't work moving forward. Today, Brazil is a new country, with new habits and customs, and believe it or not, a population that possesses an extremely elevated self-esteem. Meaning, the fledgling and rapidly growing Brazilian middle class, 52 percent of the population since 2008, is in love with itself and ready to spend. According to Goldman Sachs, more than two billion people around the world will belong to the middle-class by 2030, but the majority of Brazilians are already there.

In 2010, the United Nations Development Program's (UNDP) report, ranked Brazil among the ten worst countries in the world in terms

---

* From 2001 until 2013, Brazil's unemployment rate averaged 8.8 percent reaching an all time high of 13.1 percent in April of 2004 and a record low of 4.6 percent in December of 2012.

of income inequality, with a Gini* Index of 0.56 (one being ideal and zero being the worst), tied with Ecuador and only better than Bolivia and Haiti. Brazil is home to 31 percent of all Latin American millionaires, about five thousand people with a net worth superior of $30 million. More than 100 thousand Brazilians own financial investments of at least one million reais, or about $500 thousand. But what this report fails to include is that in 2008 the Gini index was far worse: 0.515. Since then, 2010 date indicates unemployment fell from 12.3 percent to 6.7 percent and, as mentioned earlier, it is now at 4.9 percent. In 2003 there were 49 million Brazilians living in poverty. Six years later that number plummeted to 29 million as a result of government sponsored social programs.

Brazil's primary challenge is in regard to education. In our view, the global economy has essentially become a knowledge economy. However, Brazil has not adequately invested in education, despite the commodities boon. Recently, the federal government launched several promising educational programs, such as "science without barriers," a program that finances and sends several thousand higher education students abroad in the STEM (science, technology, engineering, and math) disciplines. Sadly though, the reality today is that approximately 80 percent of all corporate professionals in Brazil do not have a college degree—one of the lowest rates in the world.

According to a United Nations Educational, Scientific and Cultural Organization (UNESCO) report, only 35 percent of Brazilians between the ages of 25 and 34 have high school diplomas, which is three times higher than those between the ages of 55 and 64 years of age. The new generation of professionals is not being educated quickly enough. Compare this data to South Korea, which planned for its economic growth by increasing the number of high school graduates from 35 to 97 percent. As of March 2013, the United States number was 75 percent. Still, in the past five years, there have never been as many Brazilians studying, with tangible results. In the past 10 years, 435 vocational schools opened and the number of universities jumped from 1,800 to almost 3,000

---

* The Gini index is a measure of statistical dispersion intended to represent the income distribution of a nation's residents. It was developed by the Italian statistician and sociologist Corrado Gini.

institutions, while the number of college students jumped 46 percent, reaching 6.5 million. By comparison, the United States has 4,495 Title IV-eligible instituations and about 20.3 million college students. As we look toward the future, despite all its shortcomings, we are looking at a much more educated workforce in Brazil.

Until now Brazilians did not believe in their country's potential and suffered from a certain inferiority complex. Now, they have several reasons to take pride in being Brazilian: the impressive economic boom of late, greater access to education and to information (Brazil is fifth in the world in Internet access, behind only China, U.S., India, and Japan), a democratization of the culture, and the recognition of Brazil as an emerging country abroad.

While there are a variety of different methodologies being used to study the relatively new field of Happiness Economics, or the efficiency with which countries convert the earth's finite resources into happiness or well-being measures. The think tank company Global Finance has ranked 151 countries across the globe on the basis of how many long, happy, and sustainable lives they provide for the people who live in them per unit of environmental output. The Global Happy Planet Index[18] (HPI) incorporates three separate indicators, including ecological footprint, or the amount of land needed to provide for all their resource requirements plus the amount of vegetated land needed to absorb all their CO_2 emissions and the CO_2 emissions embodied in the products they consume; life satisfaction, or health as well as "subjective well-being" components such as a sense of individual vitality, opportunities to undertake meaningful, engaging activities, inner resources that help one cope when things go wrong, close relationships with friends and family, belonging to a wider community; and life expectancy. According to the report results, Brazil ranks 21, while the United States is 105. (Costa Rica leads the way and Vietnam is second.) Need we say more?

CHAPTER 4

Coping With Emerging and Advanced Market Risks

Overview

For the past six years or so, advanced economies have been exposing international investors to a lot of risk, from the U.S. economy trembling over its fiscal cliff and the EU struggling to control the eurozone crisis, to Japan seemingly sunk into permanent stagnation. Hence, it would be easy to conclude that the biggest global risks, as of now, would come from these advanced economies.

Yet, that's not what Eurasia, a political risk consultancy group, argues. In its predictions for 2013,[1] the group puts emerging markets at the top of their risk rankings. That's because, they argued, the advanced economies have proved in recent years that they can manage crises. Conversely, there are several risks suggesting emerging markets will likely struggle to cope with the world's growing political pressures. Eurasia argues that

> But…with an absence of global leadership and geopolitics very much "in play," everyone will face more volatility. That's going to prove a much bigger problem for emerging markets than the developed world. In 2013, the first true post-financial crisis year, we'll start to see that more clearly.*

People tend to think of emerging markets—including the so-called BRIC nations of Brazil, Russia, India, and China—as immature states in which political factors matter at least as much as economic fundamentals for the performance of markets.

---

* Ibidem.

It was even before the recent global financial crisis that growth of emerging markets had shaken the foundations of faith in free markets, which appeared to have fully, and finally, established the dominance of the liberal economic model tested by the past success of advanced economies. The model's fundamental components are private wealth, private investment, and private enterprise. Figure 4.1 illustrates the significant growth these regions have experienced in the past decade or so.

(a) **Unprecedented**
Emerging-market share of world GDP*

% point change on previous year   % of total

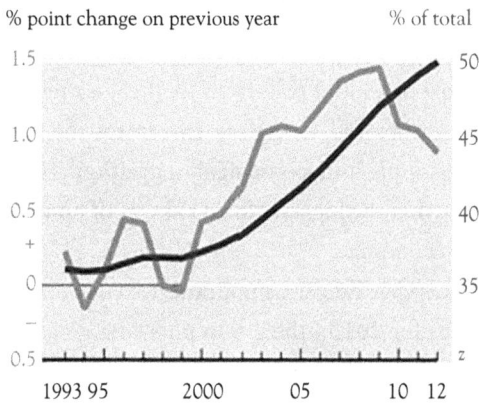

(b)   **The BRIC build-up**
GDP†, % change on previous year

BRICs   Emerging   US   G7
         markets

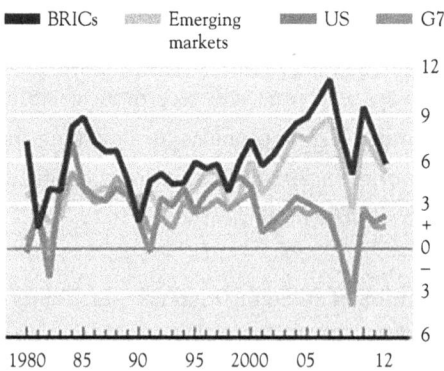

*At purchasing power parity
†Weighted by share of GDP at atpurchasing power parity

Figure 4.1 Emerging markets led by BRIC have demonstrated stronger growth than the advanced economies[2]

Source: IMF.

To combat the economic and social challenges surfaced from the global financial recession, both advanced and emerging economies have injected politics and political motivations, on a scale we haven't seen in decades, into the performance of global markets. Massive state interventions, including currency rate manipulation, inflation targeting, state capitalism, and economic nationalism in certain areas, have been accelerated in markets as world-wide governments and central banks try to stimulate growth and rescue vulnerable domestic industries and companies.

However, such a shift doesn't guarantee a panacea for all economic problems. Along with its own risks and intensified confrontation, emerging markets' most tumultuous growth model seems to have more or less reached a turning point. Growth rates in all the BRICs have dropped while the United States and EU are facing possible secular stagnation; that calls for a more thorough search for better measures and solutions.

Currency Rate

Currency war, also known as competitive devaluation of currency, is a term raised as the alarm by Brazil's Finance Minister Guido Mantega to describe the 2010 effort by the United States and China to have the lowest value of their currencies.[3]

The rationale behind a currency war is really quite simple. By devaluing one's currency it makes exports more competitive, giving that individual country an edge in capturing a greater share of global trade, therefore, boosting its economy. Greater exports mean employing more workers and therefore helping improve economic growth rates, even at the eventual cost of inflation and unrest.

The United States allows its currency, the dollar, to devalue by expansionary fiscal and monetary policies. It's doing this through increasing spending, thereby increasing the debt, and by keeping the federal funds rate at virtually zero, subsequently increasing credit and the money supply. More importantly, through "quantitative easing" (QE), it has been printing money to buy bonds, with its peak at $85 billion a month.

China tries to keep its currency low by pegging it to the dollar, along with a basket of other currencies. It keeps the peg by buying U.S. Treasuries, which limits the supply of dollars, thereby strengthening it. This keeps Chinese yuan low by comparison. More recently, the yuan has taken a

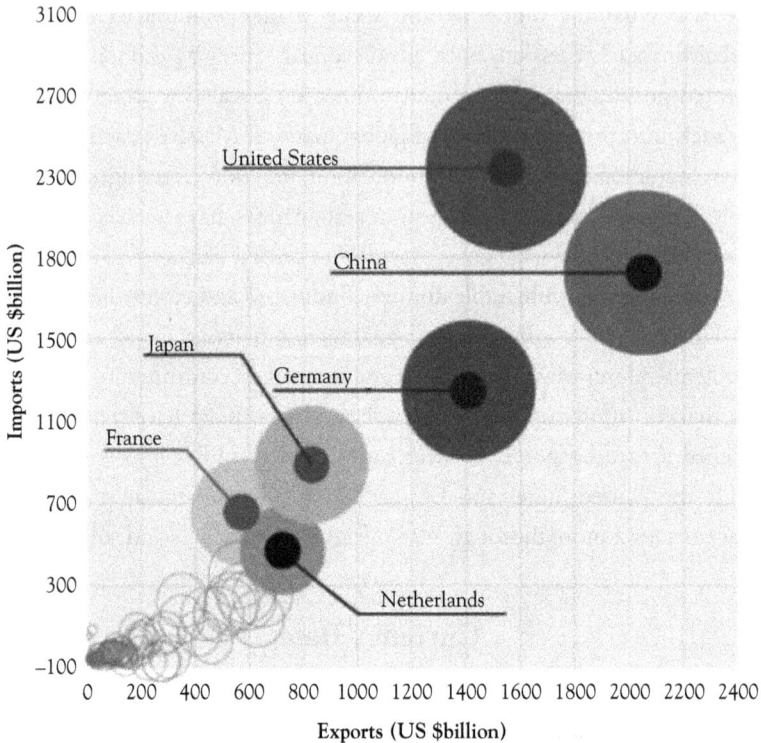

Figure 4.2 Leading export and import traders of 2012

Source: International Trade Statistics 2013 (WTO).

violent turn toward devaluation against the dollar since February 2014. Obviously, both United States and China benefitted from currency rate manipulation to secure their leading positions in international trade.

According to the WTO International Trade Statistics 2013 and as depicted in Figure 4.2, the United States was the world's biggest trader in merchandise by then*, with imports and exports totaling $3,881 billion in 2012. Its trade deficit amounts to $790 billion, or 4.9 percent of its GDP. China followed closely behind the United States, with merchandise trade totaling $3,867 billion in 2012. China's trade surplus was $230 billion, or 2.8 percent of its GDP.

---

* China replaced the United States to become the world's largest merchandise trader in 2013. Data from the U.S. Commerce Department showed on Feb 6, 2014 that the United States' combined exports and imports stood at $3.91 trillion in 2013, about $250 billion less than China's.

Through manipulation of currency rate, devaluation also is used to cut real debt levels by reducing the purchasing power of a nation's debt held by foreign investors, which works especially well for the United States. But such currency rate manipulation has invited destructive retaliation in the form of a quid pro quo currency war among the world's largest economies.

A joint statement issued by the government and the Bank of Japan (BOJ) in January 2013 stated that the central bank would adopt a two percent inflation target. Later, Haruhiko Kuroda, the BOJ's governor announced the BOJ's boldest attempt so far to stimulate Japan's economy and end years of deflation. The bank intends to double the amount of money in circulation by buying about ¥13 trillion yens in financial assets, including some ¥2 trillion yens in government bonds, every month as long as necessary. BOJ's effort together with the months of anticipation that preceded it has knocked the yen down sharply against the dollar and other major currencies (as shown in Figure 4.3) and sparked a rally

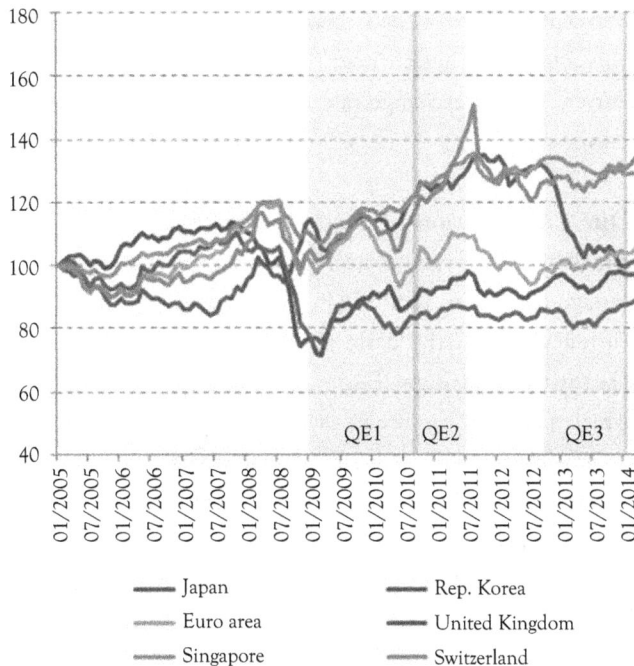

Figure 4.3 U.S. dollar exchange rates against currencies of selected countries, January 2005–March 2014. Indices of U.S. dollars per unit of national currency, 1 January 2005 = 100.

Sources: Federal Reserve Bank of St. Louis.

in Japanese shares. It also has further reignited fears of currency tensions around the globe.

The EU made its move in 2013 to boost its exports and fight deflation. The ECB, after cutting its policy rate to 0.5 percent in May, lowered its rate further to 0.25 percent on November 7, 2013. This immediately drove down the euro-to-dollar conversion rate to $1.37 dollars.

Brazil and other emerging market countries are concerned because the currency wars are driving their currencies higher, by comparison. This raises the price of commodities, such as oil, copper, and iron, that is, their primary exports. This makes emerging market countries less competitive and slows their economic growth.

In fact, India's new central bank governor, Raghuram Rajan, has criticized the United States and others involved in currency wars that they are exporting their inflation to the emerging market economies.

However, condemning the currency war and the United States, BRICS, except for China, had their currencies devaluated against the U.S. dollar after the financial crisis. (See Figure 4.3)

In currency wars, exchange rate manipulation can be accomplished in several ways:

- **Direct intervention**—Adopted by the PBOC and BOJ, in which a country can sell its own currency in order to buy foreign currencies, resulting in a direct devaluation of its currency on a relative basis.
- **Quantitative easing**—Taken by U.S. Federal Reserve, in which a country can use its own currency to buy its own sovereign debt, and ultimately depreciate its currency.
- **Interest rates**—Exercised by BOJ, Federal Reserve, and ECB in which a country can lower its interest rates and thereby create downward pressure on its currency, since it becomes cheaper to borrow against others.
- **Threats of devaluation**—Used by the United States toward China, in which a country can threaten to take any of the aforementioned actions along with other measures and occasionally achieve the desired devaluation in the open market.

An important episode of currency war occurred in the 1930s. As countries abandoned the Gold Standard during the Great Depression, they used currency devaluations to stimulate their economies. Since this effectively pushes unemployment overseas, trading partners quickly retaliated with their own devaluations. The period is considered to have been an adverse situation for all concerned as unpredictable changes in exchange rates reduced overall international trade.

Control the Currency Rate and Capital Flows

To avoid a repeat of such painful history and damage to international trade caused by ongoing currency wars, Pascal Lamy, former Director-General of the WTO, pointed out in the opening to the WTO Seminar on Exchange Rates and Trade in March 2012 that "the international community needs to make headway on the issue of reform of the international monetary system. Unilateral attempts to change or retain the status quo will not work."

The key challenge to the rest of the world is the United States policy of renewed quantitative easing, which gives both potential benefits and increasing pressure to other countries. Among the benefits would be to help push back the risk of deflation that has been observed in much of the advanced world. Avoiding stagnation or renewed recession in advanced economies, in turn, would be a major benefit for emerging markets in world trade, whose economic cycles remain closely correlated with those in the developed world (Canuto 2010). Another major plus would be to greatly reduce the threat of protectionism, particularly in the United States. The most plausible scenario for advanced country protectionism would be a long period of deflation and economic stagnation, as seen in the 1930s (Canuto and Giugale 2010).

Based on our observations, the adjustment issue has been relatively easier in other advanced economies (especially countries within the EU) that also are experiencing high unemployment and are threatened by deflation. In this situation, there could be a rationale not so much for a currency war as for a coordinated monetary easing across developed countries to help fend off deflation while also reducing the risk of big exchange rate realignments among the major developed economies (Portes 2010).

In contrast, it is more complicated for most emerging markets, such as China, that experience relatively stronger growth and higher inflationary rather than deflationary pressures. In this situation, the U.S. easing poses more challenging policy choices by creating added stimulus for capital flows to emerging markets, flows that have already been surging since 2010, and attracted both by high short-term interest rate spreads and the stronger long-term growth prospects of emerging economies.

To put currency rate and capital flows under reasonable control with the increasing pressure from U.S. monetary easing, there are three approaches suggested by the World Bank experts (Brahmbhatt, Canuto, and Ghosh December, 2010).

First is to maintain a fixed exchange rate peg and an open capital account while giving up control of monetary policy as an independent policy instrument. This approach tends to suit smaller economies such as Hong Kong that are highly integrated both economically and institutionally with the larger economy to whose exchange rate they are pegged. It is less appropriate for larger developing countries, such as China, whose domestic cycles may not be at the same pace as the economy (in this case the United States) to which they are pegged. Importing loose U.S. monetary policy will tend to stimulate excessive domestic money growth, inflation in the goods market, and speculative bubbles in asset markets. By taking this approach, China's adjustment will occur through high inflation, the highest one among all major economies in Figure 4.4, and appreciation of the real exchange rate. Countries may attempt to avert some of these consequences by issuing domestic bonds to offset the balance of payments inflows. But this course also has disadvantages, for example, fiscal costs and a tendency to attract yet more capital inflows by pushing up local bond yields.

Second is to pursue independent monetary policies that target their own inflation and activity levels, combined with relatively flexible exchange rates and open capital accounts, which a growing number of emerging economies have been moving toward in the aftermath of the financial crises of the late 1990s. Given rising inflation pressures, the appropriate monetary policy in many emerging markets at present would likely be to tighten, which will, however, attract even more capital inflows and further appreciate exchange rates. Sustained appreciation

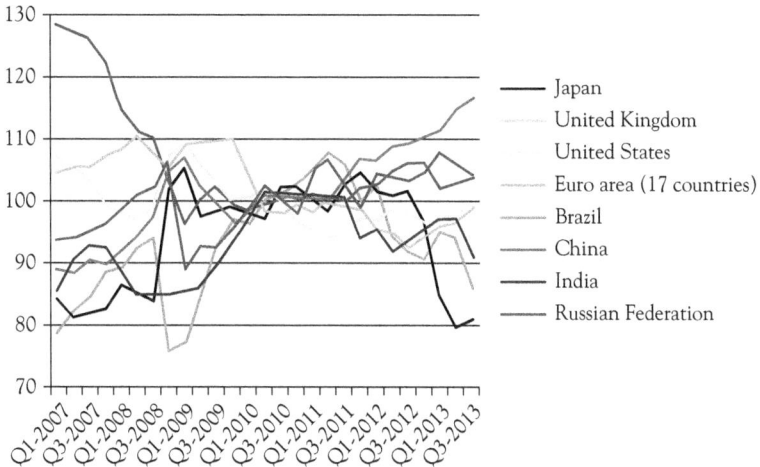

Figure 4.4 *Relative consumer price indexes, 2010=100*

Sources: OECD Main Economic Indicators (MEI) database.

raises concerns about loss of export competitiveness and could lead to contentious structural adjustments in the real economy. So countries may also fear that large appreciations will undercut their long-term growth potential.[4] A standard recommendation for countries in this position is to tighten fiscal policy (increasing the rate of taxation or cutting government spending) as a way of reducing upward pressure on local interest rates and the exchange rate.

Third is to combine an independent monetary policy with a fixed exchange rate by closing the capital account through capital controls. Such controls may sometimes be a useful temporary expedient, but they are not unproblematic, especially in the longer term.

Figure 4.5 lists some of the main types of capital controls and some evidence of their varying effectiveness. Foreign exchange taxes can be effective in reducing the volume of flows in the short term, and can alter the composition of flows toward longer-term maturities. Unremunerated reserve requirements also can be effective in lengthening the maturity structure of inflows, but their effectiveness diminishes over time. There is some evidence that prudential measures that include some form of capital control (such as a limit on bank external borrowing) may be effective in reducing the volume of capital inflows.

Types of capital controls	Volume of inflows	Composition of inflows
Foreign exchange tax	Can somewhat reduce the volume in the short term.	Can alter the composition of inflows toward longer-term maturities.
Unremunerated reserve requirements (URRs): Typically accompanied by other measures		Have been effectively applied in reducing short-term inflows in overall inflows, but their effect diminishes overtime.
Prudential measures with an element of capital control	Some evidence that prudential type controls can be effective in reducing capital inflows.	
Administrative controls: These are sometimes used in conjunction with URRs	Effectiveness depends largely on existence of other controls in the country.	

Figure 4.5 Effectiveness of capital control measures[5]

In practice, most emerging economies combine the three in varying proportions, achieving, for example, a certain degree of monetary autonomy combined with a "managed" flexible exchange rate.

It is interesting to observe two major emerging economies as points on this continuum. Brazil is an example of flexible exchange rates, independent monetary policy and high international financial integration, which is now experiencing a fluctuation in its exchange rate, and adding pressure to its competitiveness. In addition, a rising current account deficit is raising concerns about the risk of a future crisis. Under such circumstances, it is plausible for the policy makers to turn to a combination of exchange market intervention and capital flow controls to try to temper or smooth the pace of its currency appreciation. More importantly, Brazil may need to tighten fiscal policy to reduce incentives for capital inflows. Strengthening macroprudential and financial regulation as well as developing capital markets can help reduce the risk of a build-up in financial fragility and improve the efficiency of capital allocation, along with better safety nets to reduce the costs of transitional unemployment. Many of these reforms will take time to implement.

China, another member of BRIC, represents a different point with limited exchange rate flexibility, backed by heavy exchange market intervention, and some capital controls. China is experiencing the high inflation pressures in goods and asset markets predicted by the first approach offered by WTO. Chinese policy makers may understand and appreciate the potential macromanagement benefits of greater exchange rate flexibility and more monetary autonomy. But the macroeconomic management has become intertwined with deep structural imbalances—high investment relative to consumption, industry relative to services, and corporate profits relative to wages—each bolstered by vested interests and a complex political economy.

Authorities are concerned about the size and duration of transitional unemployment caused by a downsizing of the tradable goods and export sectors, which may become a threat to the social stability ranking high on their priority list. Thus the move toward macroeconomic policy reform and more exchange rate flexibility in China, though inevitable, is likely to be prolonged (Brahmbhatt, Canuto, and Ghosh December, 2010).

To echo what Lamy said at the WTO seminar, reform of the international monetary system to cease currency war and put capital flow under control takes time. Joint efforts, from advanced and from emerging economies, are needed in global platforms such as the G-20 and the World Bank to coordinate advanced countries macroprudential and financial sector regulatory reform that can help reduce the risk and improve the quality of capital flows to emerging markets. Such process would not necessarily lead to radical accomplishment, but rather incremental action, backed by sound commitment to momentous progress over the medium term.

Inflation Targeting

Inflation, a rise in the overall level of prices, erodes savings, lowers purchasing power, discourages investment, inhibits growth, fuels capital outflow, and, in extreme cases, provokes social and political unrest. People view it negatively and governments consequently have tried to battle inflation by adopting conservative and sustainable fiscal and monetary policies.

Because interest rates and inflation rates tend to move in opposite directions, central bankers have adopted *inflation targeting* to control the general rise in the price level based on such understanding of the links from the monetary policy instruments of interest rates to inflation. By applying inflation targeting a central bank estimates and makes public a projected or "target" inflation rate and then attempts to use interest rate changes to steer actual inflation toward that target. Through such "transmission mechanism," the likely actions a central bank will take to rise or lower interest rates become more transparent, which leads to an increase in economic stability.

Inflation targeting, as a monetary-policy strategy, was introduced in New Zealand in 1990. It has been very successful in stabilizing both inflation and the real economy. As of 2010, as shown in Figure 4.6, it has been adopted by almost 30 advanced and emerging economies.[6]

Inflation targeting is characterized by (1) an announced numerical inflation target, (2) an implementation of monetary policy that gives a major role to an inflation forecast and has been called forecast targeting, and (3) a high degree of transparency and accountability.

A major advantage of inflation targeting is that it combines elements of both "rules" and "discretion" in monetary policy. This "constrained discretion" framework combines two distinct elements: a precise numerical target for inflation in the medium term and a response to economic shocks in the short term.[7]

Inflation Targeting With Advanced Economies

There are a number of central banks in more advanced economies—including the ECB, the U.S. Federal Reserve (Fed), the BOJ, and the Swiss National Bank—that have adopted many of the main elements of inflation targeting. Several others are moving toward it. Although these central banks are committed to achieving low inflation, they do not announce explicit numerical targets or have other objectives, such as promoting maximum employment and moderate long-term interest rates, in addition to stablizing prices.

In popular perception, and in their own minds, central bankers were satisfied with inflation targeting as an effective tool to squeeze high inflation

Targeting inflation				
Country	Inflation targeting adoption date	Inflation rate at adoption date (percent)	2010 end-of-year inflation (percent)	Target inflation rate (percent)
New Zealand	1990	3.30	4.03	1 – 3
Canada	1991	6.90	2.23	2 +/– 1
United Kingdom	1992	4.00	3.39	2
Australia	1993	2.00	2.65	2 – 3
Sweden	1993	1.80	2.10	2
Czech Republic	1997	6.80	2.00	3 +/– 1
Israel	1997	8.10	2.62	2 +/– 1
Poland	1998	10.60	3.10	2.5 +/– 1
Brazil	1999	3.30	5.91	4.5 +/– 1
Chile	1999	3.20	2.97	3 +/– 1
Colombia	1999	9.30	3.17	2 – 4
South Africa	2000	2.60	3.50	3 – 6
Thailand	2000	0.80	3.05	0.5 – 3
Hungary	2001	10.80	4.20	3 +/– 1
Mexico	2001	9.00	4.40	3 +/– 1
Iceland	2001	4.10	2.37	2.5 +/– 1.5
Korea, Republic of	2001	2.90	3.51	3 +/– 1
Norway	2001	3.60	2.76	2.5 +/– 1
Peru	2002	–0.10	2.08	2 +/– 1
Philippines	2002	4.50	3.00	4 +/– 1
Guatemala	2005	9.20	5.39	5 +/– 1
Indonesia	2005	7.40	6.96	5 +/– 1
Romania	2005	9.30	8.00	3 +/– 1
Serbia	2006	10.80	10.29	4 – 8
Turkey	2006	7.70	6.40	5.5 +/– 2
Armenia	2006	5.20	9.35	4.5 +/– 1.5
Ghana	2007	10.50	8.58	8.5 +/– 2
Albania	2009	3.70	3.40	3 +/– 1

Figure 4.6 Summary of Central Banks using inflation targeting to control inflation

Sources: Hammond 2011, Roger 2010, and IMF staff calculations.

out of their economies. Their credibility is based on keeping inflation down and therefore they always must be on guard in case prices start to soar.

This view is dangerously outdated after the financial recession. The biggest challenge facing the advanced economies' central banks today is that inflation is too low! After rebounding during the first two years of the recovery, due to United States quantitative easing and loosening monetary policy of other advanced economies, inflation in developed markets has drifted lower since mid-2011 and generally stands below central bank targets, as depicted in Figure 4.7. Given considerable slack in developed economies, however, inflation may drop further.

The most obvious danger of such low inflation is the risk of slipping into outright deflation, in which prices persistently fall. As Japan's experience in the past two decades shows, deflation is both deeply damaging and hard to escape in weak economies with high debts. Since loans are fixed in nominal terms, falling wages and prices increase the burden of paying them. Once people expect prices to keep falling, they put off buying things, weakening the economy further.[8]

This is particularly severe in the eurozone, where growth averaged −0.7 percent in the first three quarters of 2013 and annual CPI inflation fell from 2.2 percent at the end of 2012 to 0.9 percent in the year to November 2013 (see Figure 4.7). At the same time the euro has

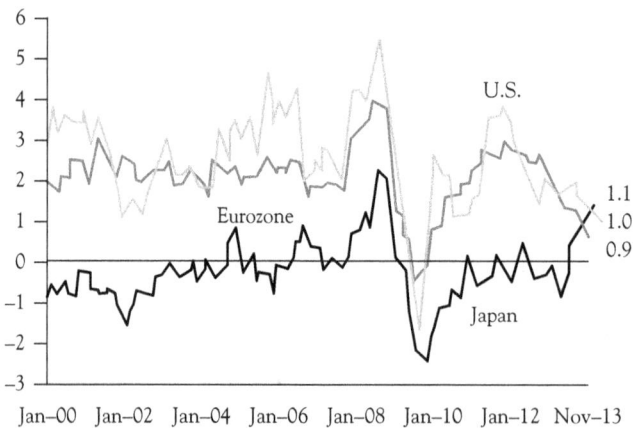

Figure 4.7 *CPI Inflation of United States eurozone, and Japan from January 2000 to November 2013 (percent, year-on-year)*

Sources: Bloomberg and QNB Group.

appreciated 8.2 percent in 2013 against a weighted basket of currencies, which is likely to be holding back inflation and growth. The ECB already cut its main policy rate from 0.5 percent to 0.25 percent in November 2013, leaving little room for further interest rate cuts.

Meanwhile, inflation in the United States has fallen to around one percent, the lowest levels since 2009 when the global recession and collapsing commodity markets dragged down prices. These low inflation rates raise the risk that the United States together with the eurozone could be entering their own deflation trap with lost decades of low growth and deflation ahead.

Interestingly enough, Japan sets a deviant example in inflation targeting, in which its central bank wants to reversely boost inflation to a set target of two percent. Since the 1990s, the Japanese economy has languished in a weak state of feeble growth and deflation that has persisted into this century. From 2000 to May 2013, annual inflation of the CPI was negative (averaging −0.3 percent), while real GDP growth was less than one percent over the same period.

The Prime Minister Shinzo Abe, who came to power at the end of 2012, introduced a raft of expansionary economic policies known as "Abenomics" (see Chapter 3), which included a two percent inflation target and buying about ¥13 trillion in financial assets (some ¥2 trillion in government bonds) every month as long as necessary. Together with heavy spending on public infrastructure and an active policy the Japanese yen was weakened.

Japan's economy has turned. Growth has averaged 3.1 percent so far in 2013 and inflation rose from −0.3 percent in the year in May to 1.1 percent in the year in October. This puts it above inflation in both the United States and eurozone for the first time this century. Rising Japanese inflation is a direct consequence of expansionary economic policies introduced in 2013, which could help the country escape from the lost decades of low growth and deflation from the real estate crash of 1989 until today. Abenomics including a surge of inflation is likely to have contributed significantly to Japan's improving economic performance.

The current situation in United States and eurozone calls for a continuation and possibly acceleration of unconventional monetary policy to offset the dangers that deflation could pose on an already weak recovery.

The experience of Japan provides a useful historical precedent. It is likely that the ECB will engage in unconventional monetary policies to provide stimulus by extending its long-term refinancing operations (LTROs), which provide unlimited liquidity to EU banks in exchange for collateral at low interest rates. The ECB must also stress that its target is an inflation rate close to two percent for the eurozone as a whole, even if that means higher inflation in Germany.

The United States is still buying $55 billion worth of bonds a month after its recent cut of $10 billion per month in April 2014, and will maintain its current policy rate at essentially zero for "a considerable time after the asset purchase program ends." If inflation continues to slow, QE tapering could take even longer to be implemented. Meanwhile, the Fed also can change its forward guidance as it just did to reduce the "threshold" below which unemployment must fall even further from 6.5 percent to 6 percent or below before interest rates are raised.[9]

Inflation Targeting With Emerging Economies

In emerging markets the inflation picture looks quite different. With unemployment rates hovering around long-term averages, these economies appear to be operating near their full potential. Correspondingly, emerging-markets consumer price inflation has been low since 2012 and has edged higher in recent months. In the aggregate, consumer price weighted emerging markets inflation ticked up to 4.2 percent year-over-year in September 2013, compared with 4.1 percent in August and 4 percent at the end of 2012 (see Figure 4.8). The sequential trend inflation rate (three months over three months, seasonally-adjusted annual rate) has risen more sharply since midyear, reaching 5.5 percent in September 2013.[10]

The concern for emerging-market economies is high inflation together with potential slower growth. Inflation has started to pick-up in emerging markets during 2013, even as growth has fallen short of expectations. Growth looks particularly disappointing when compared with figures from before the 2008 financial crisis. A poorer growth-inflation trade-off suggests that economic potential in emerging markets has slowed considerably. This observation is a particular worry in the largest emerging markets, including China, India, and Brazil. All have been growing at

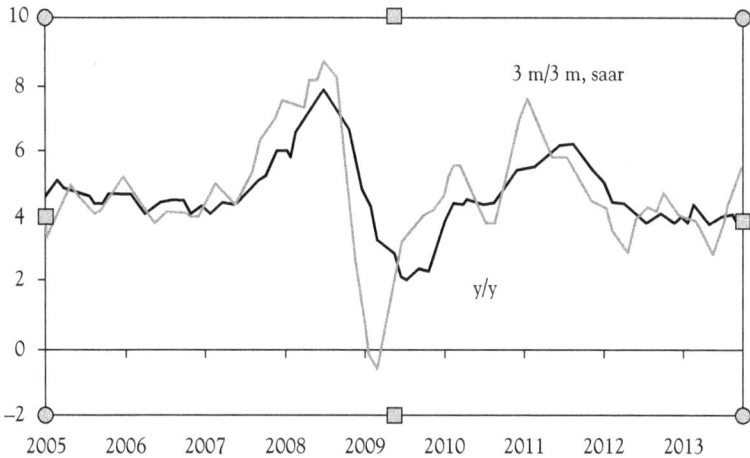

Figure 4.8 Emerging markets consumer price (percent)

Sources: J.P. Morgan Asset Management, data through September 2013.

poor rates compared with previous years, but inflation hasn't fallen significantly during the past year.

Inflation targeting has been successfully practiced in a growing number of countries over the past 20 years, and many more countries are moving toward this framework. Although inflation targeting has proven to be a flexible framework that has been resilient in changing circumstances including during the recent global financial crisis, emerging markets must assess their economies to determine whether inflation targeting is appropriate for them or if it can be tailored to suit their needs. Facing the unique challenge of high inflation with slow growth, emerging economies may include currency rate and other alternatives, along with interest rates, to play a more pivotal role in stabilizing inflation.

State Capitalism

The spread of a new sort of state capitalism in the emerging world is causing increasing attention and problems. As a symbol of state owned enterprises (SOEs), over the past two decades, striking corporate headquarters have transformed the great cities of the emerging markets. China Central Television's building resembles a giant alien marching across Beijing's skyline; the gleaming office of VTB, a banking powerhouse, sits at the heart of Moscow's new financial district; the 88-story PETRONAS Towers, home to Malaysia's oil company, soars above Kuala Lumpur. These are all monuments to the rise of a new kind of *Hybrid Corporation*, backed by the state but behaving like a private-sector multinational.[11]

State capitalism is described usually as an economic system in which commercial and economic activity is undertaken by the state, with management and organization of the means of production in a capitalist manner including the system of wage labor, and centralized management.[12]

State capitalism also can refer to an economic system where the means of production are owned privately but the state has considerable control over the allocation of credit and investment, as in the case of France during the period of dirigisme. Alternatively, state capitalism may be used similar to state monopoly capitalism to describe a system where the state intervenes in the economy to protect and advance the interests of large-scale businesses. This practice is often claimed to be in contrast with the ideals of both socialism and laissez-faire capitalism.[13] In 2008, the term was used by U.S. National Intelligence Council in "Global Trends 2025: A World Transformed" to describe the development of Russia, India, and China.

Marxist literature defines state capitalism as a social system combining capitalism, in which a wage system of producing and appropriating surplus value, with ownership or control by a state. Through such combination, a state capitalist country is one where the government controls the economy and essentially acts like a single huge corporation, extracting the surplus value from the workforce in order to invest it in further production.

State-directed capitalism is not a new idea. It's remote roots can be traced back to the East India Company. After Russia's October Revolution in 1917, using Vladimir Lenin's idea that Czarism was taking a "Prussian path" to capitalism, Nikolai Bukharin identified a new stage in the development of capitalism, in which all sectors of national production and all important social institutions had become managed by the state. He officially named this new stage as "state capitalism."[14]

Rising powers have always used the state to drive the initial growth, for example, Japan and South Korea in the 1950s, or Germany in the 1870s, or even the United States after the war of independence. But these countries have eventually found the limits of such a system and thus moved away from it.

Singapore's economic model, under Lee Kuan Yew's government, is another form of state capitalism, where the state lets in foreign firms and embraces Western management ideas while owning controlling shares in government-linked companies and directs investments through sovereign wealth funds, mainly Temasek.

Within the EU, state capitalism refers to a system where high coordination between the state, large companies and labor unions ensure economic growth and development in a quasicorporatist model. Vivien Schmidt cites France and, to a lesser extent, Italy as prime examples of modern European State capitalism.[15]

The leading practitioners of state capitalism nowadays are among emerging markets represented by China and Russia—after Boris Yeltsin's reform. The tight connection between its government and business is so obvious, whether in major industries or major markets. The world's ten biggest oil-and-gas firms, measured by reserves, are all state-owned. State-backed companies account for 80 percent of the value of China's stock market and 62 percent of Russia's. Meanwhile, Brazil has pioneered the use of the state as a minority shareholder together with indirect government ownership through the Brazilian National Development Bank (BNDES) and its investment subsidiary (BNDESPar).[16]

State capitalists like to use China's recent successes against the United States and EU's troubles in the financial crises. They argue that state owned enterprises have the best of both worlds: the ability to plan for the future, but also respond to fast-changing consumer tastes. State capitalism has been successful at producing national champions that can compete globally. Two-thirds of emerging-market companies that made it onto the Fortune 500 list are state-owned, and most of the rest enjoy state support of one sort or another. Chinese companies are building roads and railways in Africa, power plants and bridges in South-East Asia, and schools and bridges in the United States. In the most recent list of the world's biggest global contractors, compiled by an industry newsletter, Chinese companies held four of the top five positions. China State Construction Engineering Corporation has undertaken more than 5,000 projects in about 100 different countries and earned $22.4 billion in revenues in 2009. China's Sinohydro controls more than half the world's market for building hydropower stations.[17]

In 2009, just two Chinese state-owned companies, namely China Mobile and China National Petroleum Corporation, made more profits ($33 billion) than China's 500 most profitable private companies combined. In 2010, the top 129 Chinese SOEs made estimated net profits of $151 billion, 50 percent more than the year before (in many cases helped by near-monopolies). In the first six months of 2010, China's four biggest state commercial banks made average profits of $211 million a day.

Under state capitalism, governments can provide SOEs and companies under their indirect control with the resources that they need to reach global markets. One way is by listing them on foreign exchanges, which introduces them to the world's sharpest bankers and analysts. Meanwhile, they can also acquire foreign companies with rare expertise that produces global giants. Shanghai Electric Group enhanced its engineering knowledge by buying Goss International for $1.5 billion and forming joint ventures with Siemens and Mitsubishi. China's Geely International gained access to some of the world's most advanced car-making skills through its acquisition of Volvo for $1.8 billion.*

Governments embrace state capitalism because it serves political as well as economic purposes. Especially, during the recent recession, it puts vast financial resources within the control of state officials, allowing them access to cash that helps safeguard their domestic political capital and, in many cases, increases their leverage on the international stage.

Risks Associate With State Capitalism

Dizzied by the strength of state capitalism demonstrated through the recent financial crisis, it is easy for outside investors to become blind to the risks posed by the excessive power of the state. Companies are ultimately responsible not to their private shareholders but to the government, which not only owns the majority of the shares but also controls the regulatory and legal system. Such inequality creates a lot of risks for investors.

There is striking evidence that state-owned companies are less productive than their private competitors. An OECD paper in 2005 noted that the total factor productivity of private companies is twice that of state companies. A study by the McKinsey Global Institute in the same

---

* Ibidem.

COPING WITH EMERGING AND ADVANCED MARKET RISKS   101

year found that companies in which the state holds a minority stake are 70 percent more productive than wholly state-owned ones.

Studies also show that SOEs use capital less efficiently than private ones, and grow more slowly. The Beijing-based Unirule Institute of Economics argues that, allowing for all the hidden subsidies such as free land, the average real return on equity for state-owned companies between 2001 and 2009 was −1.47 percent.* SOEs typically have poorer cost controls than regular companies. When the government favors SOEs, the others suffer. State giants soak up capital and talent that might have been used more efficiently by private companies.

SOEs also suffer from "principal-agent problem," which indicates the tendency of managers, as agents who run companies, to put their own interests prior to the interests of the owners who are the principals. This problem is getting more severe under state capitalism. Politicians who can control or influence the nomination of SOE executives may have their own agenda while being too distracted by other things to exercise proper oversight. Boards are weak, disorganized, and full of insiders.

For example, the Chinese party state exercises power through two institutions: the State-Owned Assets Supervision and Administration Commission (SASAC) and the Communist Party's Organization Department. They appoint all the senior managers in China Inc. Therefore, even the most prestigious top executives of China's SOEs are cadres first and company men second, who naturally care more about pleasing their party bosses than about the market and customers. Ironically, China's SOEs even have successfully attempted to make them pay more dividends to their major shareholder, that is, the state.

Politicians under state capitalism have far more power than they do under liberal capitalism, which creates opportunities for rent seeking and corruption on the part of the SOE elite. State capitalism suffers from the misfortune that it has taken root in countries with problematic states. It often reinforces corruption because it increases the size and range of prizes for the victors. The ruling parties of SOEs have not only the government apparatus but also huge corporate resources at their disposal.

In China, where its long history combines with a culture of *guanxi* (relationships) and corruption, the PBOC, China's central bank, estimates

---

* Ibidem.

that between the mid-1990s and 2008, some 16,000 to 18,000 Chinese officials and SOE executives made off with a total of $123 billion. Russia has the nepotism and corruption among a group of "bureaugarchs," often-former KGB officials, who dominate both the Kremlin and business. Other BRIC countries suffer from the similar problems. Transparency International, a campaigning group, ranks Brazil 72nd in its corruption index for 2013, with China 80th, India 94th, and Russia an appalling 127th. In contrast, as Figure 4.9 shows, advance economies favoring a free market model score much better than their emerging market counterparts under state capitalism.

State capitalism also stems the rise of various degrees of globalization as it shackles the flow of money, goods, ideas, information, people, and services within countries and across international borders. Ensuring that trade is fair is harder when some companies enjoy the direct or indirect support from a national government. Western politicians are beginning to lose patience with state-capitalist powers that rig the system in favor of their own companies.

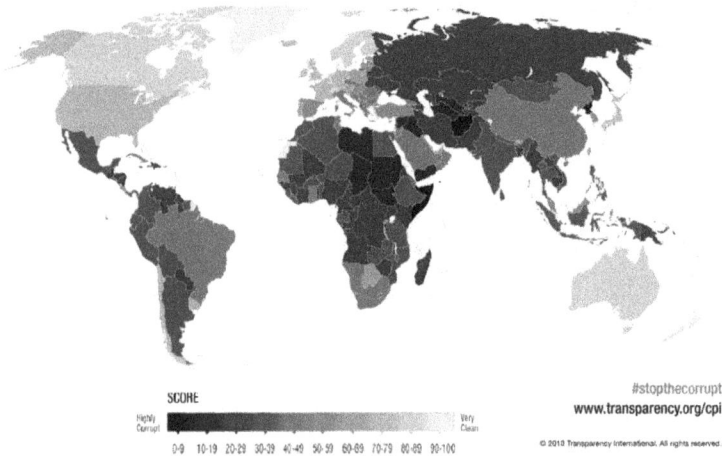

Figure 4.9 Corruption Perceptions Index 2013

Source: Transparency International Transparency International*

---

* More detail information available at http://cpi.transparency.org/cpi2013/results/

More worrying is the potential for capriciousness. State-capitalist governments can be unpredictable with scant regard for other shareholders. Politicians can suddenly step in and replace the senior management or order SOEs to pursue social rather than business goals. In 2004, China's SASAC and the Communist Party's Organization Department rotated the executives of the three biggest telecoms companies. In 2009, they reshuffled the bosses of the three leading airlines. In 2010, they did the same to the heads of the three largest state oil companies, each of which is a Fortune 500 company.

Response to State Capitalism

Will state capitalism completely reverse globalization's progress? Ian Bremmer, the founder and president of the Eurasia Group, indicated that it is highly unlikely. Despite the relatively high growth of emerging markets after the global financial crisis, it has not proven that government engineered growth can outstrip the expansion of well-regulated free markets over the long run. States like China and Russia will face tremendous pressures as internal issues contradict their development. Recently, we witnessed the terrible environmental price China continues to pay for its growth. And Russia's vulnerable reliance on Vladimir Putin, at the expense of credible governing institutions, put their economic resilience to the test. A free market does not depend on the wisdom of political officials for its dynamism; that's the primary reason it will almost certainly withstand the state capitalist challenge.

However, the financial crisis and advanced countries' apparent responsibility for it may ensure the growth of state capitalism over the next several years. The future of this path will depend on a range of factors, including any wavering of Western faith in the power of free markets, the U.S. administration's capacity to kick-start its economy growth, the ability of Russian government's dependence on oil exports to withstand the pain inflicted by prices drop, the Chinese Communist Party's ability to create jobs and maintain tight control of its own people, and dozens of other variables. In the meantime, corporate leaders and investors must recognize that free market capitalism is no longer the unchallenged international economic paradigm and that politics will have a profound impact on the performance of markets for many years to come.

Increasingly, multinational companies and international traders are operating in an environment where they have to pay much more attention to politics, and they can't invest purely on the basis of where the markets may be attractive.[18]

Economic Nationalism

In the good old days, growth in trade and cross-border investment brought prosperity and development. Globalization appeared to deliver rising living standards for all and there was no conflict. Leaders of nations could simultaneously support the architecture of globalization while taking the plaudits for prosperity at home. That's all changed. As English statesman Lord Palmerston noted: "nations have no permanent friends or allies, they only have permanent interests."

Nations led by politicians, who are primarily interested in strengthening their political capitals by serving and protecting their most powerful constituents (the local voters, political benefactors, or powerful industries and interest parties), naturally try to help boost their domestic economies rather than making choices with the global economy in mind. In the aftermath of the global financial crisis, these interests dictated a body of policies that emphasized domestic control of the economy, labor, and capital formation, even if this required the reversal of the trend to greater global integration and a return to economic nationalism.[19]

The financial crisis inevitably revealed that integration reduces the effectiveness of a nation's economic policies, unless other nations take coordinated action. Governments' initial reaction to the global financial crisis was to pour large amounts of government spending in a competitive rather than cooperative way to bailout its own economy first, as shown in Figure 4.10.

As it became clear that the recession would last longer than originally anticipated, governments started to throw up barriers to trade and investment meant to keep local workers employed through the next election. Economic nationalism leads to the imposition of tariffs and other restrictions on the movement of labor, goods, and capital. The United States tacked a 127 percent tariff on to Chinese paper clips; Japan put a 778 percent tariff on rice. Protection is worse in the emerging world, as shown

	Discretionary fiscal stimulus	Financial assistance (excluding guarantees)	Total crisis fighting
UK	1.6	32.1	33.7
Japan	4.2	26.5	30.6
China	5.8	21.3	27.1
US	3.8	21.4	25.2
Russia	5.4	16.7	22.1
Brazil	1.2	13.3	13.5
India	1.2	9.6	10.8
Germany	3.6	4.2	7.8
France	1.5	2.7	4.2
Italy	0.3	0.7	1.0

Figure 4.10 *2009–2010 fiscal stimulus and financial bailouts, percentage GDP (Select G-20 countries)*

Source: IMF, 2009b.

in Figure 4.11. Brazil's tariffs are, on average, four times higher than the United States, and China is three times higher.

Besides tariffs, big emerging markets like Brazil, Russia, India, and China have displayed a more interventionist approach to globalization that relies on industrial policy and government-directed lending to give domestic sellers more advantages. Industrial policy enjoys more respectability than tariffs and quotas, but it raises costs for consumers and puts more efficient foreign firms at a disadvantage. The Peterson Institute estimates local-content requirements cost the world $93 billion in lost trade in 2010.[20]

For advanced economies, government procurement policies also favor national suppliers. "Buy American" campaigns as seen in the recent U.S. presidential election and preferential policies are used to direct demand. Safety and environmental standards are used to prevent foreign products penetrating national markets. According to Global Trade Alert, a monitoring service, at least 400 new protectionist measures have been put in place each year since 2009, and the trend is on the increase.

Another obvious move in economic nationalism is through capital markets. Nations facing financial difficulties with high levels of

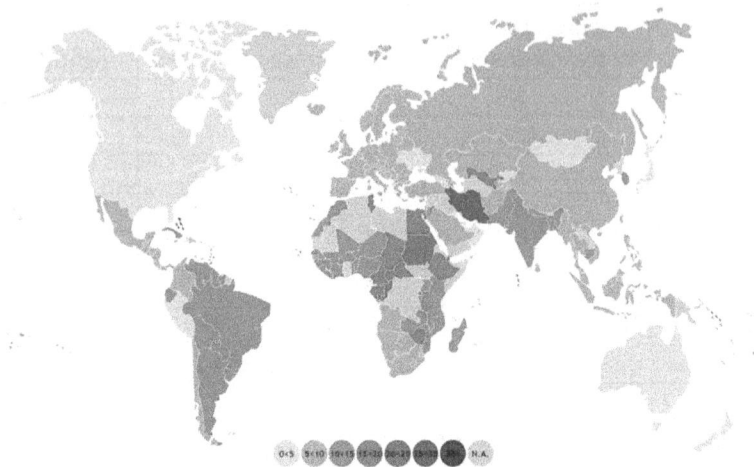

Figure 4.11 2012 Year of MFN applied tariff

Source: © World Trade Organization 2013.

government debt seek to limit capital outflows. These would prevent depositors and investors withdrawing funds to avoid potential losses from sovereign defaults. In Europe, there was a tendency for a breakdown in the common currency and redenomination of investments into a domestic currency.

In Cyprus, explicit capital controls designed to prevent capital flight were implemented. On the other hand, low interest rates and weak currencies in developed economies have led to volatile and destabilizing capital inflows into emerging nations with higher rates and stronger growth prospects. Brazil, South Korea, and Switzerland have implemented controls on capital inflows.

As a result, global capital flows fell from $11 trillion in 2007 to a third of that in 2012. The decline happened partly for cyclical reasons, but also because regulators of nations who saw banks' foreign adventures end in disaster have sought to gate their financial systems.

Political tension and national security can make existing economic nationalism more complicated and intensified. Mr. Snowden first revealed the existence of the clandestine data mining program of U.S. National Security Agency (NSA) in June 2013. The NSA involves U.S. firms in the IT and telecoms space. Basically, it ensures U.S. firms operate under certain kinds of rules in connection with the U.S. government and the military industrial complex. Snowden's revelations provoked a storm in the Chinese media and added urgency to Beijing's efforts to use its market power to create indigenous software and hardware.

As a consequence, U.S. technology companies including Cisco Systems immediately face new challenges in selling their goods and services in China as fallout from the U.S. spying scandal, which caused relations between Beijing and Washington to be strained by Mr. Snowden's reports of American espionage, starts to take a toll. Cisco Systems warned its revenue would dive as much as 10 percent in the fourth quarter of 2013, and keep dipping until after the middle of 2014, in part due to a backlash in China after Snowden's revelations about U.S. government surveillance programs. Beijing may be targeting Cisco in particular as retaliation for Washington's refusal to buy goods from China's Huawei Technologies Co, a telecommunications equipment maker that the United States claims is a threat to national security because of links to the Chinese military.

Response to Economic Nationalism

Economic nationalism may offer near-term pain relief but, as a political response to economic failure, it only risks locking in that economic failure for the long term. The world learned from the Great Depression that protectionism makes a bad situation worse.

Trade encourages specialization, which brings prosperity. Economic cooperation encourages confidence and enhances security. Global capital markets, for all their problems, allocate money more efficiently than local ones.

In December 2013, the WTO sealed its first global trade deal after almost 160 ministers gathered on the Indonesian island of Bali and agreed to reforms to boost world commerce. Tense negotiations followed 20 years of bitter disputes. At the heart of the agreement were measures to ease barriers to trade by reducing import duties, simplifying customs procedures, and making those procedures more transparent to end years of corruption at ports and border controls.

"For the first time in our history, the WTO has truly delivered," WTO chief Roberto Azevedo told exhausted ministers after the long talks. "This time the entire membership came together. We have put the 'world' back in World Trade organization," he said. "We're back in business … Bali is just the beginning."

China, a key member of BRICS, also started to respond to the challenge in the right way. On December 2nd of 2013, the PBOC issued a set of guidelines on how financial reform will proceed inside the new Shanghai Free Trade Zone (SFTZ). This 29 sq. km (about 18 sq. miles) enclave, created three months earlier, has been trumpeted by Li Keqiang, the country's prime minister, as a driver of economic reform under his new administration.

To boost cross-border investment and trade, the PBOC wants to allow firms and individuals to open special accounts that will enable them to trade freely with foreign accounts in any currency. Selected foreign institutional investors may be allowed to invest directly in the Shanghai stock market. Interest rates may be liberalized for certain accounts at designated firms inside the SFTZ, which would open a new window of globalization and free capital market in China.

Conclusion

As mentioned at the beginning of this chapter, the BRIC economies are contributing less to global growth. In 2008 they accounted for two-thirds of world GDP growth. In 2011 they accounted for half of it, in 2012 a bit less than that. The IMF sees growth staying at about that level for the next five years. Goldman Sachs predicts that, based on an analysis of fundamentals, the BRICs share will decline further over the long term.

Other emerging markets will pick up some of the slack including the "Next 11" which includes Bangladesh, Indonesia, Mexico, Nigeria, and Turkey, to name a few. Although there are various reasons to think that this N-11 cannot have an impact on the same scale as that of the BRICs, emerging markets other than BRIC will play a vital role in the future. Advanced economies will continue to lose their share which will contribute to a general easing of the pace of world growth,[21] as shown in Figure 4.12.

Past a peak?

World GDP, % change on previous year*

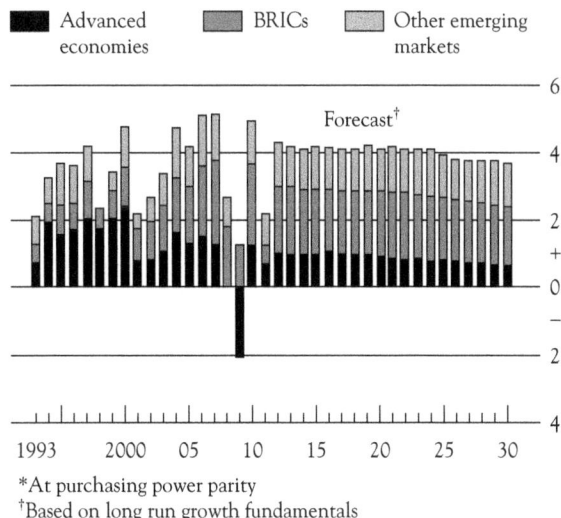

■ Advanced   ▨ BRICs   ▨ Other emerging
   economies   markets

Forecast†

```
6
4
2
+
0
–
2
4
```

1993   2000   05   10   15   20   25   30

*At purchasing power parity
†Based on long run growth fundamentals

Figure 4.12 Emerging markets led by BRIC have demonstrated stronger growth than the advanced economies

Source: Goldman Sachs.

Internationally, lower growth could focus leaders on increased cooperation and a new push for liberalization, which will mitigate the risks, as
discussed, of currency war, inflation targeting, state capitalism, and economic nationalism. A predicted slowdown could bring new consensus to
global trade talks as witnessed in Bali in December 2013. More deals that
address nontariff trade barriers, and especially those on trade in services,
could yield bigger benefits down the road.

CHAPTER 5

Global Economies at War

Overview

More than half a decade has passed since the financial crisis hit, traversing the global economy very rapidly, confirming just how interconnected the world has become as ideas, information, capital, and new technologies have streamed across borders with increasing ease. Nevertheless, the lack of sustained financial crisis response has made it clear just how fractured the international political landscape has become, as advanced and emerging economies' diverging interests make global coordination ever more difficult. Hence, despite sustained globalization, and in some cases because of it, we are seeing a growing vacuum of global leadership, as well as traditional geopolitical risks, which consequently are on the rise.

This chapter attempts to address key global issues for tomorrow that demand our attention today. It provides an overview of many of the most volatile, significant, and misunderstood developments reshaping the global geopolitical landscape, from the growing global vulnerability of public and private institutions to the increasing impact of public opinion and protest.

As James Rickards (2011) argues the world is amidst a full-blown currency war, and assuming this is true, there are several undercurrents between advanced economies and emerging markets to which we need to be attentive, beginning with the U.S.-China dynamics, the relations between China and the Russian Federation, and more broadly the rest of Asia. We also attempt to address the significant shifts in the Middle East, and the unconventional energy revolution in North America that is primed to reshape global energy markets and the world's balance of power. The central focus of this chapter, aside from developing awareness that global economies are at war, is the fact that the world, more than ever before, is constantly and rapidly changing, and international business professionals must seek guidance on how to understand the key players in the evolving global landscape.

Such trends have gained momentum in shaping global trade, especially among advanced economies and emerging markets, leading to a host of new challenges to policymakers worldwide, as well as international traders and multinational corporations. In a world where the international agenda is coming undone, local and shorter-term challenges take precedence for policymakers and international business leaders. That itself is an issue, as longer-term risks go unaddressed and loom larger. Furthermore, we have seen an increased vulnerability of elites, as a host of new voices, whether from the voting booth in advanced economies, populist parties, growing middle classes in emerging markets, or through new technologies, have put added strain on leaders who are increasingly *takers* rather than *makers* of policy.

Economies at War

Since 2010, government officials from the G-7 economies have been very concerned with the potential escalation of a global economic war. Not a conventional war with fighter jets, bullets, and bombs, but rather, a "currency war." Finance ministers and central bankers from advanced economies worry that their peers in the G-20, which also includes several emerging economies, may devalue their currencies to boost exports and grow their own economies at their neighbors' expense.

Brazil led the charge, being the first emerging economy to accuse the United States of instigating a currency war in 2010, when the U.S. Federal Reserve bought piles of bonds with newly created money. From a Chinese perspective, with the world's largest holdings of U.S. dollar reserves, a U.S. lead currency war based on dollar debasement is an American act of default to its foreign creditors. So far the Chinese have been more diplomatic, but their patience is waning.

These two countries are not alone, as depicted in Figure 5.1. Several other emerging markets, such as Saudi Arabia, Korea, Russia, Turkey, and Taiwan also have been impacted by a weak dollar. Quantitative easing (QE) made investors flood emerging markets with hot money in search of better returns, which consequently lifted their exchange rates. But Brazil

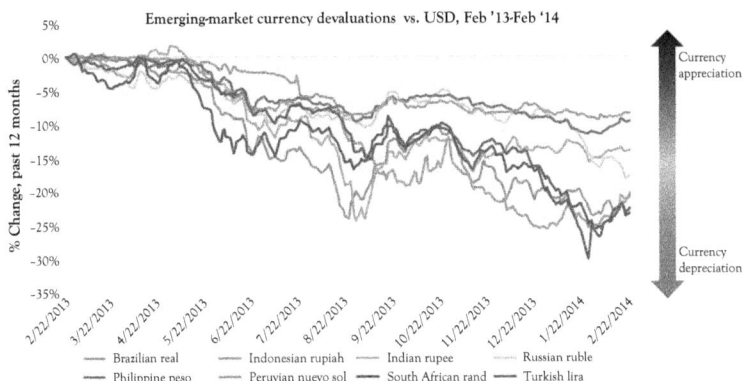

Figure 5.1 Emerging market currencies inflated by weak dollar

Source: Frontier Strategy Group.

was not alone, as Japan's prime minister Shinzo Abe has reacted to the QEs in the United States and pledged bold monetary stimulus to restart growth and vanquish deflation in the country.

As advanced economies, like the three largest world economies— United States, China, and Japan respectively—try to kick-start their sluggish economies with ultra low interest rates and sprees of money printing, they are putting downward pressure on their currencies. The loose monetary policies are primarily aimed at stimulating domestic demand, but their effects spill over into the global currency world.

Japan faces charges that it is trying to lower the value of its currency, the yen, to stimulate its economy and get an edge over other countries. The new Japanese government is trying to get Japan, which has been in recession, moving again after a two-decade bout of stagnant growth and deflation. Hence, it embarked on an economic course it hopes will finally jump-start the economy. The government coerced the Bank of Japan to accept a higher inflation target, which triggered speculation that the bank will create more money. The prospect of more yen in circulation has been the main reason behind the yen's recent falls to a 21-month low against the dollar and a near three-year record against the euro.

Since Abe called for a weaker yen to bolster exports, the currency has fallen by 16 percent against the dollar and 19 percent against the euro. As the yen falls, its exports become cheaper, and also those of its neighbors,

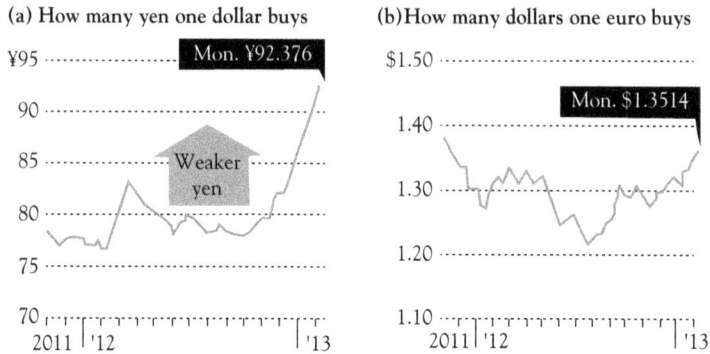

(a) How many yen one dollar buys

¥95 .... Mon. ¥92.376

90 ....

85 .... Weaker ....

80 .... yen ....

75 ....

70
2011 '12   '13

(b)How many dollars one euro buys

$1.50 ....

                    Mon. $1.3514
1.40 ....

1.30 ....

1.20 ....

1.10 ....
2011 '12   '13

Figure 5.2 Central banks in the United States and Japan have flooded their economies with liquidity

Source: WSJ Market Data Group.

such as of Asian neighbors South Korea and Taiwan. At the same time the exports for those countries further afield in Europe, become relatively more expensive. As depicted in Figure 5.2, central banks in the United States and Japan have flooded their economies with liquidity since mid-2012 and into 2013, causing the both the yen and the dollar to weaken against other major currencies.

In our opinion, common sense could prevail, putting an end to the dangerous game of beggar (and blame) thy neighbor. After all, the IMF was created to prevent such races to the bottom, and should try to broker a truce among foreign exchange competitors. The critical issues in the United States, as well as China and Japan, stem from ineffective public policy, but more so a failed and destructive economic policy. These policy errors are directly responsible for the opening salvos of the currency war clouds now looming overhead.*

So far, Europe has felt the most impact of the falling yen. At the height of the eurozone's financial crisis in 2012, the euro was worth $1.21, which was potentially benefitting big exporters like BMW, AUDI,

---

* Our opinion expressed here is from the point of you of international trade and currency exchange as far as it affects international trade, and not from the geopolitical and economic aspects of the issue. We approach the issue of currency wars not from the theoretical, or even simulation models undertaken from behind a desk in an office, but from the point of view of practitioners engaged in international business and foreign trade, on the ground, in four different countries.

Mercedes, or Airbus. However, at the time of this writing in December 2013, the euro is at $1.38 even though the eurozone is still the laggard of the world economy.

Across the 17-strong euro area a recovery has been under way following a double-dip recession lasting 18 months, but it is a feeble one. For 2013 as a whole GDP still will continue to fall by 0.4 percent (after declining by 0.6 percent in 2012), but it is expected to rise by 1.1 percent in 2014.[1] A rise in the value of the euro has to do with the diminishing threat of a collapse of the currency, will do little to help companies in the eurozone—and barely help it regrow.

Chinese policymakers reject the conventional thinking proposed by advanced economies. How about the yen's extraordinary rise over the last 40 years, from JPY360 against the dollar at the beginning of the 1970s to about JPY102 today?* Not to mention that despite this huge appreciation, Japan's current account surplus has only gotten bigger, not smaller. They could also argue that the United States' prescription for China's economic rebalancing, a stronger currency and a boost to domestic demand, was precisely the policy followed by the Japanese in the late-1980s, leading to the biggest financial bubble in living memory and the 20-year hangover that followed.

Furthermore, the demand by the United States, which is backed by the G-7 to revalue the renminbi, in our view, is a policy of the U.S.'s default. During the Asian crisis in 1997 to 1998, advanced economies, under the auspices of the IMF, insisted that Asian nations, having borrowed so much, should now tighten their belts. Shouldn't advance economies be doing the same? In addition, Chinese manufacturing margins are so slim that significant change in exchange rates could wipe them out and force layoffs of millions of Chinese. As it is, labor rates are already climbing in China, further squeezing margins. Lastly, a revaluation of the yuan would only push manufacturing to other cheaper emerging markets, such as Vietnam, Cambodia, Thailand, Bangladesh, and other lower paying nations without improving the advanced economies trade deficits.

Some G-7 policymakers believe these criticisms grumbles are overdone; arguing that the rest of the world should praise the United States

---

* As of December 2013.

and Japan for such monetary policies, suggesting the eurozone should do the same. The war rhetoric implies that the United States and Japan are directly suppressing their currencies to boost exports and suppress imports, which in our view is a zero-sum game, which could degenerate into protectionism and a collapse in trade.

These countries, however, do not believe such a currency devaluation strategy will threaten trade. Rather, their belief seems to be that as central banks continue to lower their short-term interest rate to near zero, exhausting their conventional monetary methods in the process, they must employ unconventional methods, such as QE, or try to convince consumers that inflation will arise. The goal is to lower real (inflation-adjusted) interest rates. If so, inflation should be rising in the United States and in Japan, which according to Figure 5.3 it is.

Over the past decade, Japan has seen the consumer price index (CPI) for most periods hover just below the zero-percent inflation line (see Figure 5.3). The notable exceptions were in 2008, when inflation rose as high as two percent, and in late 2009, when prices fell at close to a two percent rate. The rise in inflation coincided with a crash in capital spending. The worst period of deflation preceded an upturn. Of course, the graph does not provide enough data to conclude causal effects, but

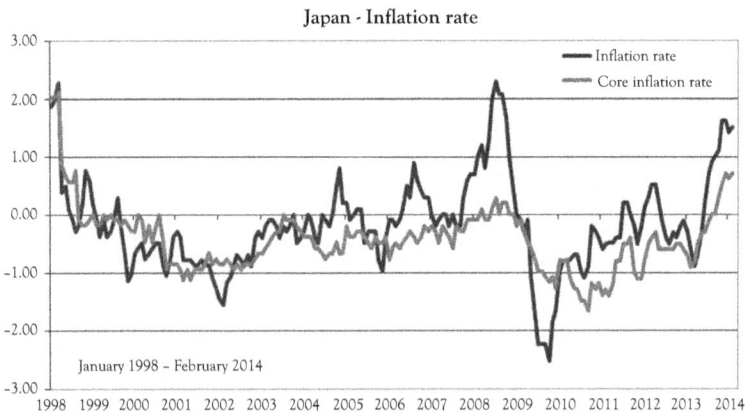

Figure 5.3 Japan's inflation rate has been climbing since 2010 as a result of economic stimulus

Source: Datastream, Natixis AM, Trading Economics,[2] Japan's Ministry of Internal Affairs & Communications.

it seems, however, that the relationship between growth and Japan's mild deflation may be more complicated than the Great Depression-inspired deflationary spiral narrative suggests. The principal goal of this policy was to stimulate domestic spending and investment, but lower real rates usually weaken the currency as well, and that in turn tends to depress imports. Nevertheless, if the policy is successful in reviving domestic demand, it will eventually lead to higher imports.

At least that's the idea behind the argument. The IMF concluded that the United States' first rounds of QE boosted its trading partners' output by as much as 0.3 percent. The dollar did weaken, but that became a motivation for Japan's stepped-up assault on deflation. The combined monetary boost on opposite sides of the Pacific has been a powerful elixir for global investor confidence, if anything, to move hot-money emerging markets where the interests were much higher than in advanced economies.

The reality is that most advanced economies have overconsumed in recent years. It has too much debt. Rather than dealing with the debt by living a life of austerity or accepting a period of relative stagnation these economies want to shift the burden of adjustment onto its creditors, even when those creditors are relatively poor nations with low per capita incomes. This is true not only for China but also for many other countries in Asia and in other parts of the emerging world. During the Asian crisis in 1997 to 1998, Western nations, under the auspices of the IMF, insisted that Asian nations, having borrowed too much, should tighten their belts. However, the United States doesn't seem to think it should abide by the same rules. Better to use the exchange rate to pass the burden onto someone else than to swallow the bitter pill of austerity.

Meanwhile, European policymakers, fearful that their countries' exports are caught in this currency war crossfire, have entertained unwise ideas such as directly managing the value of the euro. While the option of generating money out of thin air may not be available to emerging markets, where inflation tends to remain problematic, limited capital controls may be a sensible short-term defense against destabilizing inflows of hot money. Figure 5.4 illustrates how the inflows of hot-money leaving advanced economies in search of better returns on investments in emerging markets have caused these markets to significantly outperform advanced (developed) markets.

FTSE All-World indices
rebased in $ terms

Figure 5.4 In 2009 emerging markets significantly outperformed advanced (developed) economies

Source: FTSE All-World Indices.

Currency War May Cause Damage to Global Economy

As more countries try to weaken their currencies for economic gain, there may come a point where the fragile global economic recovery could be derailed and the international financial system thrown into chaos. That's the reason financial representatives from the world's leading 20 industrial and developing nations spent most of their time during the G-20 summit in Moscow in September 2013.

In September 2011, Switzerland took action to arrest the rise of its currency, the Swiss franc, when investors, looking for somewhere safe to store their cash from the debt crisis afflicting the 17-country eurozone, saw in the Swiss franc the traditional instrument to fulfill that role. The Swiss intervention was viewed as an attempt to protect the country's exporters.

In our view, policymakers are focusing on the wrong issue. Rather than focus on currency manipulation, all sides would be better served to hone in on structural reforms. The effects of that would be far more beneficial in the long run than unilateral United States, China, or Japan currency action, and more sustainable. The G-20 should focus on a comprehensive package centered on structural reforms in all countries, both advanced economies and emerging markets. Undeniably, exchange rates should be an important part of that package. For instance, to reduce the U.S. current-account deficits, Americans must save more. To continue to simply devalue the dollar will not be sufficient for that purpose. Likewise, China's current-account surpluses were caused by a broad set of domestic economic distortions, from state-allocated credit to artificially low interest rates. Correcting China's external imbalances requires eliminating these distortions as well.

As long as policymakers continue to focus on currency exchange issues, the volatility in the currency markets will continue to escalate. Indeed, it has become so worrisome that the G-7 advanced economies have warned that volatile movements in exchange rates could adversely hit the global economy. Figure 5.5 provides a broad view (rebased at 100 percent on August 1, 2008) of main exchange rates against the dollar.

When it became clear that Abe with his agenda of growth-at-all-costs would win Japan's elections, the yen lost more than 10 percent against the dollar and some 15 percent against the euro. In turn, the dollar dropped to its lowest level against the euro in nearly 15 months. These monetary

Figure 5.5 Exchange rates against the dollar

Source: Bloomberg.

debasement strategies are adversely impacting and angering export-driven countries such as Brazil, and many of the BRICS, ASEAN, CIVETS, and MENA blocs. But these strategies also are stirring the pot in Europe. The eurozone has largely remained quiet regarding monetary stimulus and now finds itself in the invidious position of having a contracting economy and a rising currency.

These currency moves have shocked BRICS countries as well as other emerging-market economies, including Thailand. The G-20 is clearly divided between the advanced economies, including the UK, the United States, Japan, France, Canada, Italy, and Germany, and emerging countries such as Russia, China, South Korea, India, Brazil, Argentina, and Indonesia. Top leaders of Russia, South Korea, Germany, Brazil, and China have expressed their concern over the currency moves, which drive up the value of their currencies and undermine the competitiveness of their exports. If they decide to enter the playing field, like Venezuela, which has devalued its currency by 32 percent, the world would plunge into competitive devaluations. Competitive devaluations would lead to run-away inflation or hyperinflation. Nobody will win with these types of currency wars.

James Rickards, author of *Currency Wars: The Making of the Next Global Crisis*, expects the international monetary system to destabilize and collapse. In his views, "there will be so much money-printing by so many central banks that people's confidence in paper money will wane, and inflation will rise sharply."[3]

If policymakers truly want to ward off this currency war, then it is a matter of doing what was done in 1985 with the Plaza Accord.* This time, however, we will need a different version, as it will not be about the United States and the then G-5 at the time, in 1985. It will have to be an *Asian Plaza Accord* under the support and auspices of the G-20. It should be about the Asian export led and mercantilist leadership agreeing among them. The chances of this happening, of advanced economies seeing the

---

* The Plaza Accord was an agreement between the governments of France, West Germany, Japan, United States, and the United Kingdom, to depreciate the U.S. dollar in relation to the Japanese yen and German deutsche mark by intervening in currency markets. The five governments signed the accord on September 22, 1985 at the Plaza Hotel in New York City.

necessity of it, or these economies relinquishing its powers in any meaningful way, are not possible under current political strategies.

Currency War Means Currency Suicide

(Special contribution by Patrick Barron*)

What the media calls a "currency war," whereby nations engage in competitive currency devaluations in order to increase exports, is really "currency suicide." National governments persist in the fallacious belief that weakening one's own currency will improve domestically produced products' competitiveness in world markets and lead to an export driven recovery. As it intervenes to give more of its own currency in exchange for the currency of foreign buyers, a country expects that its export industries will benefit with increased sales, which will stimulate the rest of the economy. So we often read that a country is trying to "export its way to prosperity."

Mainstream economists everywhere believe that this tactic also exports unemployment to its trading partners by showering them with cheap goods and destroying domestic production and jobs. Therefore, they call for their own countries to engage in reciprocal measures. Recently Martin Wolfe in the Financial Times of London and Paul Krugman of the New York Times both accused their countries' trading partners of engaging in this "beggar-thy-neighbor" policy and recommended that England and the United States respectively enter this so-called "currency war" with full monetary ammunition to further weaken the pound and the dollar.

I, Patrick, am struck by the similarity of this currency-war argument in favor of monetary inflation to that of the need for reciprocal trade agreements. This argument supposes that trade barriers against foreign goods are a boon to a country's domestic manufacturers at the expense of foreign manufacturers.

---

* Patrick Barron is a private consultant in the banking industry. He teaches in the Graduate School of Banking at the University of Wisconsin, Madison, and teaches Austrian economics at the University of Iowa, in Iowa City, where he lives with his wife of 40 years. We recommend you to visit his blog at http://patrick-barron.blogspot.com/ or contact him at PatrickBarron@msn.com.

Therefore, reciprocal trade barrier reductions need to be negotiated, otherwise the country that refuses to lower them will benefit. It will increase exports to countries that do lower their trade barriers without accepting an increase in imports that could threaten domestic industries and jobs. This fallacious mercantilist theory never dies because there are always industries and workers who seek special favors from government at the expense of the rest of society. Economists call this "rent seeking."

A Transfer of Wealth and a Subsidy to Foreigners

As Patrick explained in his article *"Value in Devaluation?"*[4] inflating one's currency simply transfers wealth within the country from nonexport related sectors to export related sectors and gives subsidies to foreign purchasers.

It is impossible to make foreigners pay against their will for the economic recovery of another nation. On the contrary, devaluing one's currency gives a windfall to foreigners who buy goods cheaper. Foreigners will get more of their trading partner's money in exchange for their own currency, making previously expensive goods a real bargain, at least until prices rise.

Over time the nation which weakens its own currency will find that it has "imported inflation" rather than exported unemployment, the beggar-thy-neighbor claim of Wolfe and Krugman. At the inception of monetary debasement the export sector will be able to purchase factors of production at existing prices, so expect its members to favor cheapening the currency. Eventually the increase in currency will work its way through the economy and cause prices to rise. At that point, the export sector will be forced to raise its prices. Expect it to call for another round of monetary intervention in foreign currency markets to drive money to another new low against that of its trading partners.

Of course, if one country can intervene to lower its currency's value, other countries can do the same. So the ECB wants to drive the euro's value lower against the dollar, since the U.S. Federal Reserve has engaged in multiple programs of quantitative easing. The self-reliant Swiss succumbed to the monetary debasement Kool-Aid last summer when its sound currency was in great demand, driving its value higher, and making exports more expensive. Lately the head of the Australian central bank hinted that the country's mining sector needs a cheaper Aussie dollar to boost exports. Welcome to the modern version of currency wars, also known as, currency suicide.

There is one country that is speaking out against this madness: Germany. But Germany does not have control of its own currency. It gave up its beloved deutsche mark for the euro, supposedly a condition demanded by the French to gain their approval for German reunification after the fall of the Berlin Wall. German concerns over the consequences of inflation are well justified. Germany's great hyperinflation in the early 1920s destroyed the middle class and is seen as a major contributor to the rise of fascism.

As a sovereign country Germany has every right to leave the European Monetary Union (EMU) and reinstate the deutsche mark (DM). I, Patrick, would prefer that it go one step further and tie the new DM to its very substantial gold reserves. Should it do so, the monetary world would change very rapidly for the better. Other EMU countries would likely adopt the deutsche mark as legal tender, rather than reinstating their own currencies, thus increasing the DM's appeal as a reserve currency.

As demand for the deutsche mark increased, demand for the dollar and the euro as reserve currencies would decrease. The U.S. Federal Reserve and the ECB would be forced to abandon their inflationist policies in order to prevent massive repatriation of the dollar and the euro, which would cause unacceptable price increases.

In other words, a sound deutsche mark would start a cascade of virtuous actions by all currency producers. This Golden Opportunity should not be squandered. It may be the only noncoercive means to prevent the total collapse of the world's major currencies through competitive debasements called a currency war, but which is better and more accurately named currency suicide.

Value in Devaluation?

The euro is in trouble. That is not news. What is news is that people with deep pockets are willing to pay for economists to provide a solution.

Lord Wolfson,[5] the chief executive of Next, UK, has offered a £250,000 prize for the best way a country can exit the EMU. Five finalists for the prize were announced in March 2013, but none of the five finalists— Neil Record, Jens Nordvig, Jonathan Tepper, Catherine Dobbs, and Roger Bootle—advocates a return to sound money; all assume that new, national fiat currencies will float; and all assume that unproductive countries will benefit from devalued new currencies.

The theory is that a devalued currency will spur export-driven economic growth. Furthermore, they have little confidence that economic reforms—which they all, by the way, do recommend—will be achieved in the near term and see devaluation as a quicker alternative. But will this work? First a word about devaluation itself.

Devaluing Against Gold

Historically, devaluation of a currency referred to its relationship to gold. Gold could not be expanded in any appreciable amounts very quickly. It had to be dug up, minted, and placed into circulation at some expense over a long period of time. Coin clipping and substituting a base metal for some percentage of the gold in coins were early means of money debasement. Later, paper currencies could be expanded as quickly and as cheaply as the mint could run paper through its presses, but even this pales in comparison to these electronic times in which money can be expanded to any amount desired at the click of a mouse.

Devaluations occurred, of course, even when governments admitted that gold was money. Notable examples are the Swiss devaluation in 1936, detailed so succinctly by Mises in *Human Action*, and America's shocking 69 percent devaluation in 1934. Both of these, and others like them, were considered shameful and self-serving acts. Devaluation was tantamount to an admission of fraud. The country's central bank had printed and circulated more units of currency than it could redeem at the currency-to-gold price it had promised its trading partners. This, of course, had disastrous effects on everyone who held contractual promises to be paid in gold.

Devaluing Against Other Fiat Currencies

The devaluation advocated by many economists today is quite different in one regard. There is no commodity reserve—gold or silver, for example—against which the nation's currency is to be devalued. Modern devaluation advocates refer to the currency's value, or exchange ratio, in relation to all other fiat currencies. The exchange value between currencies is governed by purchasing-power parity, which is the simple comparison of the price levels of two countries as expressed in local currency. Nevertheless, the mechanism for devaluing is still the same as that which occurred under gold: inflation of the fiat-money supply.

For example, the central bank could give foreign buyers more local currency with which to buy local goods. This increased supply of local currency eventually works its way through the economy, raising all prices. Economists refer to this process as "importing inflation." The devaluation advocates attempt to convince their countrymen that what was once a shameful act is now a positive good. For example, the Swiss are trying to lower the value of their currency in relation to all others.

What of the proposition that taking positive steps to devalue one's own currency against all others, if it can be achieved, will actually help a country become more competitive? What have others said on this subject?

Insights From Kant, Bastiat, and Hazlitt

A policy of currency devaluation can be judged by whether or not it satisfies Immanuel Kant's "categorical imperative," which asks whether the action will benefit all men, at all places, and at all times. Certainly devaluation will benefit exporters, who can expect to make more sales. Their foreign customers get more local currency in exchange for their own. Exports increase. The exporter's position is one that is best examined by considering Frederic Bastiat's brilliant essay "That Which Is Seen, and That Which Is Not Seen" and "The Lesson" found in Henry Hazlitt's *Economics in One Lesson*.

At the instance of exchanging his money for more local currency, the foreign buyer will indeed be inclined to purchase more of the goods from the country that devalued. This we can see, and most pundits consider it a good thing. The exporter's increased sales can be measured. This is seen. But what about the importer's lost sales? Importers can expect the opposite. The local currency will buy less, and they can expect sales to fall due to the necessity of raising prices to reflect the reduced purchasing power of their local currency. How can someone measure sales that never happened? This is Bastiat's unseen.

Hazlitt would tell us to look at the longer-term effects of Bastiat's insight. What is seen is that exporters get first use of the newly created money and buy replacement factors of production at current prices. The increased profits from the higher sales enrich them, because they are the early receivers of the money. But how about those who get the money much later, such as wholesalers, or not at all, such as retirees?

Over time the new money causes all prices to rise, even the exporter's factors of production. The benefits to the exporter of the monetary intervention have slowly evaporated. The costs of his factors of production have risen. His sales start to fall back to preintervention levels. What can he do except lobby the government for another shot of monetary expansion to give his customers even more local currency with which to buy his products?

Monetary Expansion Creates the Boom-Bust Cycle

Even this increase in overall prices and their redistributive effects is not the entire story. The increase in the nation's money supply will cause the boom-bust business cycle. The Wolfson Prize finalists, who see historical evidence in the beneficial effects of devaluation, have misinterpreted the boom phase. For example, Jonathan Tepper writes "in August 1998, Russia defaulted on its sovereign debt and devalued its currency. The expected catastrophe didn't happen." Later he writes, "Argentina was forced to default and devalue in late 2001 and early 2002. Despite dire predictions, the economy did extraordinarily well." But these are merely the expected and temporary appearances of the boom phase caused by monetary expansion. Not only does the bankrupt nation shed itself of its debt and get to keep its ill-gotten gains; its expansionist monetary policy touches off a speculative boom. Neither Russia nor Argentina has built sustainable, capitalist economies.

The Exporter as Wealth-Transfer Agent

It should be clear that there is no net benefit to the country that drives down the purchasing power of its currency through monetary expansion. The only reason the exporter makes more sales is that the buyer of the exporter's goods gets a lower price. This lower price was not the result of manufacturing efficiencies, but of a subsidy—a transfer of wealth—from some in the exporting country to the foreign purchaser of the goods. With each successive monetary expansion, wealth is funneled to the exporter, his employees, and others who get the money early in the expansion phase. All others are harmed. In effect, his fellow citizens who are the late receivers of the new money have subsidized the exporter's sales. The exporter is the unseen means by which the transfer is affected. The nation as a whole is worse off; it is not more competitive.

Delaying Real Reform in a Fruitless "Race to the Bottom"

Politicians and their professional economist supporters are doing their fellow citizens an injustice by pursuing devaluation as a quick and easy means to improve national competitiveness. The source of real competitive advantage is through liberal reform of economic policies that reward industriousness in a people, to protect their property and even that of foreigners from confiscatory taxation, and encourage savings. Over time the country's capital base in relation to its population will increase; an increase in capital per capita, as economists say will raise real prosperity through increased worker productivity. Instead of forthrightly pursuing economic reform, which one must admit will be difficult, politicians and their professional-economist supporters are fomenting a "race to the bottom," by which each country tries to boost exports via competitive devaluations against all others. The nation's capital base will slowly dwindle through the backdoor export subsidy made possible through monetary debasement.

The Moral Hazard of the Welfare State

There is nothing preventing any member of the EMU from becoming more competitive right now. All that is required is willingness to lower prices. As the common medium of exchange, the euro reveals uncompetitive economic structures. So why do those countries wish to become more competitive, but refrain from lowering prices? The answer is the welfare state. In an unhampered market economy, there is no structural unemployment. All who wish to work can do so, because there is never a dearth of work to be done. But the welfare state removes the cost of pricing one's labor or one's goods and services too high. One might say that the welfare state underpins structural rigidities in an economy, such as labor laws, licensing, and so on, by removing the cost of market interventions. Devaluation does not address this underlying problem; therefore, devaluation will not cure a country's lack of competitiveness.

Conclusion

Devaluation means monetary expansion. The new money must enter the economy somewhere, for example, payments to exporters. The ensuing bubble is misinterpreted as a sign of the success of devaluation, but the well-known deleterious effects of a rising price level, income redistribution, and malinvestment accompany the bubble. As the prices for exporters' factors of production rise and the benefits of devaluation fade away, there will be calls for more money expansion. If more than one country pursues this policy, there ensues a disastrous race to the bottom.

The solution is sound money. Sound money reveals bad economic policy and forces each country to live within its means. Governments will come under pressure to liberalize their economies and shed themselves of the parasitic destroyers of wealth. Devaluation retards this process.

CHAPTER 6

The Rebalance of Global Trade

Overview

The global trade imbalance has been made abundantly clear by the ongoing global economic malaise. In our view, the United States should be comforted, not flustered, if the dollar's use as the sole global reserve currency were to come to an end, as some pundits believe may soon happen. The global financial crisis of 2007 has not yet been resolved, and China is yet to face the worst of its effects. German domestic policies postunification were as much responsible for the eurozone debt crisis as any domestic factors in the affected countries.

Consequently, very likely the EU's debt crisis will continue to affect Spaniard and European economies and politics, probably leading Spain and other countries to leave the euro due to lack of a strong fiscal union or a transformation of Germany's economic model. As of the summer of 2014, the ECB, during the first week of June, became the largest bank to announce they'd charge banks a negative interest rate to deposit their excess reserves at the central bank. This effective makes the banks pay the ECB to hold their money there rather than the banks earning interest on their deposits. The goal was to discourage banks from hoarding money at the ECB, and instead send it flowing back out to the borrowers and businesses that will stimulate the economy and raise inflation. In turn this would depreciate the euro. As the euro drops in value, eurozone exports should become cheaper and consequently, more globally competitive.

While we believe ECB's strategy in setting a negative interest rate is a bit drastic, with a very melodramatic optics, we do not think such strategy will have much stimulative effect than the already set low rate. Money is always very fungible across borders and across the ECB. To discourage banks from keeping their excess reserves on the ECB balance sheet, the ECB is in effect rewarding banks that increase their private lending with access to cheap funds. That's been tried before in the UK without significant success. In our view, the most concerning factor of ECB's strategy is the very notion of negative interest rate. If negative interest rates cut into banks' margins, surely these banks will try to pass those negative rates onto their customers, which is not a good prognostic for a typical European with a modest bank account. Banks may decide to alienate their customer base, but while they may not transfer those negative rates onto their customers, they may still transfer the cost and just call it something else, such as a new fee structure. Even if it were to happen, however, most customers, especially retail customers, would likely be reluctant to move their money around from one bank to another. Nonetheless, the fear that depositors may remove their money from the banking system entirely may keep central banks from ever making rates highly negative.

China's Rebalancing

China's rebalancing, when it suitably begins, will see GDP growth rates fall to below 6 percent and will average around 4.5 percent for a decade or so, but this will not be a disaster for China. Nonetheless, trade tensions around the world are set to rise until global imbalances are resolved. For instance, back in March 2013, the Wuxi subsidiary of Suntech Power, one of the world's largest producers of solar panels, defaulted on a bond payment of more than $500 million. The company, once praised and feared by Western analysts, went into technical bankruptcy. Such insolvency of Wuxi Suntech and its counterparts in other industries is an example of the massive policy challenges that China still needs to confront before the end of this decade. China's solar-panel industry is illustrative because it's a classic example of massive investment outstripping demand.

What is really going on? The major problem is that household consumption in China accounts for only around 38 percent of China's GDP. In other words, consumers have not begun picking up the economy's slack, as they must, if they are to fuel economic growth now that the country's investment-led model is reaching its limits. Chinese household consumption as a share of GDP is barely half that of the United States, where it typically accounts for about 70 percent of economic activity, and significantly less than the prevailing rate (approaching 60 percent in recent years) of other large economies, such as Brazil, France, Germany, and India.

As the Chinese government recognizes, China's economy must rebalance by reducing its reliance on investment and increasing consumption. Doing so while maintaining growth and stability requires both economic and political changes. We already have some preliminary evidence that economic changes are under way; political changes are harder to forecast, but the probability is certainly higher than it was in the past. Firms and executives must consider the likelihood of changes on both fronts when crafting China strategies for the next decade. That means understanding the likely promise—and peril—of China's great rebalancing.

As argued by Yasheng Huang,* a professor at the Massachusetts Institute of Technology (MIT) in the United States,

> There is no guarantee that rebalancing [in China] will succeed. Part of the problem is that the politics associated with it— boosting the income of Chinese households at the expense of state-owned companies and other large investment-oriented entities—is actually more complicated than the economics. But one thing is certain. China is rapidly reaching the point of diminishing economic and political returns from its investment-driven model, which is headed for change one way or another: either through a proactive rebalancing, with reforms and policy adjustments, or a forced rebalancing precipitated by rising stresses in and beyond the financial system. So far, the signs are encouraging that the new leadership is serious about changing China's growth model, and this is reason enough for global firms that have benefited from China's investment boom to rethink their strategies for the years ahead.[1]

---

* Dr. Huang is a professor at the Massachusetts Institute of Technology's (MIT) Sloan School of Management, where he founded and heads the China Lab and the India Lab, which provide consulting services to small and midsize enterprises in China and India, respectively.

Although most of the aforementioned paragraphs are opinions we, the authors, share and are not at all in line with what one typically reads or hears on the financial or mainstream press. Much of it has been forecasted originally by Peking University Professor Michael Pettis.* Professor Pettis bases much of his research on fairly simple economic accounting identities concerning the relationship between any country's domestic savings and investment rates, production and consumption rates, and external current and capital accounts. Building off these, he developed a theory, documented in his book, with often misunderstood other theories, explanations, and predictions for what went wrong internationally before the 2008 financial crisis, what has been going on since, and where things are likely to head in the future. A key area of his argument is that any domestic policy which affects the relationship between savings and investment or production and consumption has a trade effect, whether or not it is intended as such.

Therefore, the likely path to more sustainable levels of trade deficits remains far less clear. Consider the potential global impact of populist cries for protectionist trade policies ostensibly aimed at easing the difficult transition to more sustainable trade and debt balances. In the event of a trade war, which we discussed in Chapter 5 and is already happening, we will all lose. Perhaps even more unsettling is how these consequences would most likely manifest across nations.

The evidence presented in this chapter suggests that countries like China, which depend heavily on total trade in relation to their overall economy, could suffer most severely. This evidence further suggests that instead of pursuing short-term quick fixes that would exacerbate the malady, global policymakers must work together to establish a long-term path to more sustainable trade and debt balances.

Current Patterns of Global Imbalances

Many take as fact that the current pattern of global imbalances, or the large and persistent trade deficits and surpluses across different parts of the world, ultimately unsustainable, is due to China and ASEAN consuming

---

* In his recent book *The Great Rebalancing: Trade, Conflict, and the Perilous Road Ahead for the World Economy.*

too little and saving too much. Since the global economy is a closed trading system, trade deficits and surpluses across all national economies must always sum exactly zero. Therefore, because one part of the world saves too much and runs trade surpluses means other parts of the world, particularly the United States, must run trade deficits.

However, just because deficits and surpluses are tightly interconnected, it does not mean that trade surpluses in China or ASEAN have been responsible for the United States and EU trade deficits. In addition, China's high level of savings might be dynamically-welfare optimizing for its citizens. Note also that private enterprise in China might find self-accumulation the only way to generate investment funds.

The fact remains that countries with a current account surplus, as depicted in Figure 6.1, must also be those with exports in excess of imports, as shown in Figure 6.2. The range of imbalances among these nations has widened dramatically in recent decades, leading to a very unsustainable path. Notice in Figure 6.1 that Switzerland, Germany, and

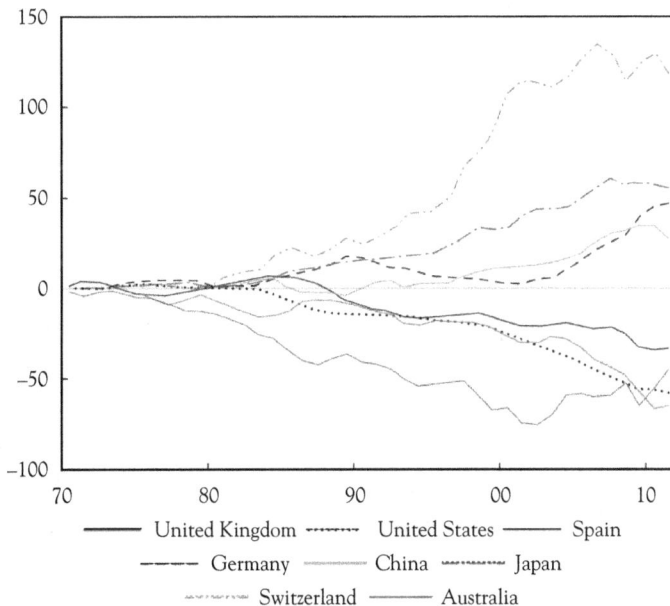

Figure 6.1 Cumulative current accounts as a percentage of GDP, 1970–2010

Source: CFA Institute.[2]

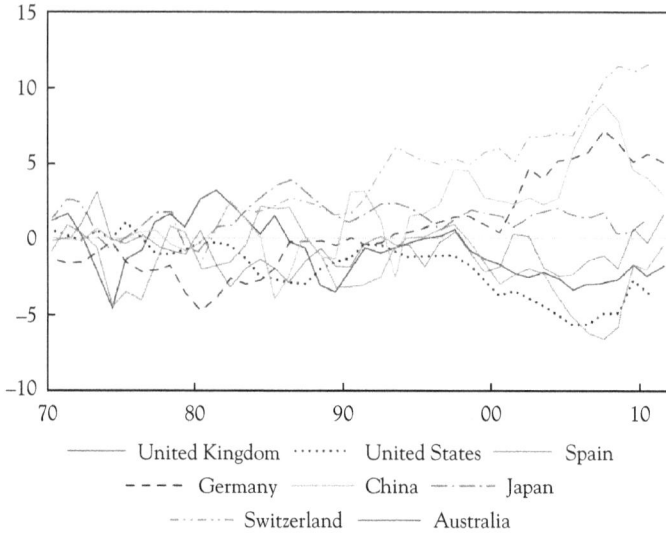

Figure 6.2 *Net exports as a percentage of GDP, 1970–2010*

Source: CFA Institute.*

China currently enjoy the largest net trade surpluses, while the United States, the UK, and Spain have the largest net deficits.

The magnitude of trade deficits matters because a country with an ongoing trade deficit is, by definition, reducing its foreign assets or borrowing. Not as well understood is that global trade patterns are financed by *gross* asset flows, not *net* asset flows. Hence, a country must have sufficient gross foreign assets to finance any trade imbalance on an ongoing basis. Undeniably, these gross asset financial flows grease the skids of global trade. Practically speaking, trade deficits must be paid for by either selling down gross assets or increasing gross liabilities by selling debt.

Despite the many theories and conjectures offered, the global economy continues to struggle as it attempts to recover, slowly and painfully, from the financial crisis it entered in 2007. According to the IMF's July 2012 report, world output growth–expressed at market exchange rates–will be roughly 2.5 percent in 2013 and about 0.5 percent faster in 2014. These rates of growth are concerning, and are far slower than those that preceded the crisis, although they are still positive. Meanwhile, China's economic

---

* Ibidem.

growth continues to sputter, even if at a lower rate. The euro is still under threat, and the United States is still combating serious trade disadvantages.

In our view, the EU's underlying problem is not budget deficits or even unsustainable debt; these are mainly symptoms. The main problem with the EU is the huge divergence in costs between the core and the periphery. In the past decade costs between Germany and some of the peripheral countries have diverged by anywhere from 20 to 40 percent. This divergence has made the latter uncompetitive and has resulted in the massive trade imbalances within Europe.

Trade imbalances, of course, are the obverse of capital imbalances, and the surge in debt in peripheral Europe, which is debt owed ultimately to Germany and the other core countries, was the inevitable consequence of those capital flow imbalances. While EU's policymakers alternatively worry over fiscal deficits, surging government debt, and collapsing banks, there is almost no prospect of them resolving the European crisis until they address the divergence in costs. Of course, if they don't resolve this problem, the problem will be resolved for them in the form of a break-up of the euro.

There is no doubt that trade deficits and surpluses narrowed significantly during this so-called *great recession*.* The economic activity in the advanced economies, mainly the G-7 nations, fell by 5 percent, while the number of unemployed people around the world surged by more than 30 million.[3] The global economy contracted by 0.8 percent in 2009, but it rebounded strongly in the next two years as central banks around the world–led by the U.S. Federal Reserve–embarked on massive monetary stimulus programs.

As depicted in Figure 6.3, the situation was so dire that in November of 2010, at the G-20 meeting in Seoul, the United States and other G-7 countries running high external deficits challenged those countries that maintain surpluses, specifically China, Germany, and Japan, along with other smaller emerging countries, to pick up the slack in global demand.[†] Predictably, this effort brought no tangible results.[†]

---

* The great recession refers to the global contraction from December 2007 to June 2009 that resulted in the world economy shrinking for the first time since 1945. The Great Recession was so-called because its severity and depth made comparisons with the Great Depression of the 1930s inevitable.

[†] Ibidem.

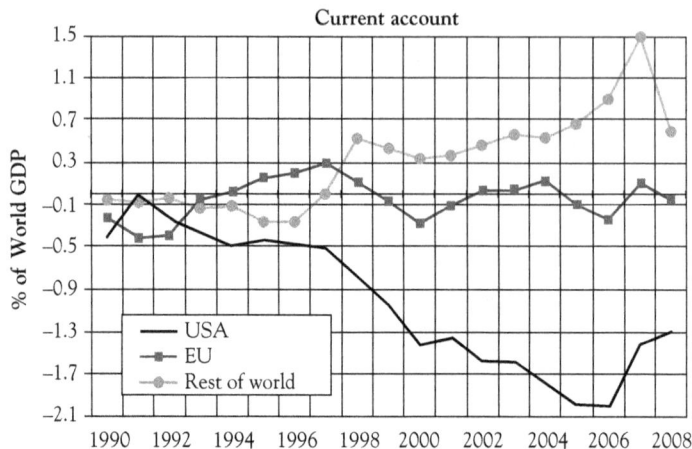

Figure 6.3 *The imbalance of the global economy as a result of the great recession*

Source: IMF.[4]

Rebalancing the Global Economy May Not Be the Solution

Although we believe a global rebalance is to some extent necessary to reduce trade deficits and surpluses, we argue that too much emphasis on that may not be healthy for the global economy. Focusing too much on rebalancing the global economy can actually be ill advised. Mind you, this is not a book on international economics; none of the authors are economists. But from the point of view of international trade and foreign affairs, global rebalance should be viewed as an idea and an overall goal, and not as a task or a mission.

For starters, emerging markets remain heavily dependent on con-sumer demand in the United States and Western Europe. If this con-sumer demand grows more slowly in the future, due to the unwinding of household debts, the influence of higher risk premium on investment, and the effect of rising national debt on government expenditures, would the export-led emerging market economies continue to grow? The answer to this question is critical, as it directly impacts strategies that will need to be in place to stimulate domestic demand for the four billion people in the emerging markets.

In the same way, assuming a rebalancing of the global trade is a realistic strategy. What would be the impact of such rebalancing trade flows across the different emerging markets, such as the ASEAN, CIVETS, MENA, and BRICS? Who is more likely to gain or lose from such rebalancing, and what should the policy response, according to these countries' different economic structures, degrees of openness, and sociopolitical institutions look like?

Furthermore, assuming global trade and capital flows were rebalanced sustainably, what implications would this have for the future of reserve currencies around the world? Can the U.S. dollar retain its reserve currency status while enabling global financial capital to flow to the most profitable investment opportunities and global trade to flow where it is needed most? Lastly, what reserve currency regime is required for sustainable trade and capital flows? These questions are not easily answerable. In our view, U.S. policymakers should forget punitive tariffs against Chinese imports; letting China grow rich might do the trick.

Global Economy is Already Undergoing Rebalancing

While Michael Pettis[5] argues that the global economy is already undergoing a critical rebalancing, he points out that the severe trade imbalances impelled on the recent financial crisis was the result of unsuccessful policies that distorted the savings and consumption patterns of some nations, mainly the G-7.* Pettis cautions about the yet to be seen consequences of these destabilizing policies, predicting severe economic dislocations in the upcoming years. He warns of a lost decade for China, the breaking of the Euro, and a continuing decline of the U.S. dollar, all with long-lasting effects.

In Pettis' views, there are a myriad of causes for his dismal global outlook and economic prospect. He points to China's maintenance of massive investment growth by artificially lowering the cost of capital, which he warns to be unsustainable. He worries that Germany is endangering the euro by favoring its own development at the expense of its neighbors' states. He also argues the U.S. dollar's role as the world's reserve currency burdens the U.S. economy. Pettis suggests that while many of these various imbalances may seem unrelated, including the U.S. consumption splurge, the surging debt in Europe, China's investment debauch, Japan's long stagnation, and the commodity boom in Latin America, they are all

---

* Ibidem.

closely tied together. This tie makes any attempt to rebalance the global economy impossible, unless each of the domestic issues (for both G-7 and G-20) are resolved. Moreover, he argues that it will be impossible to resolve any issue without forcing a resolution for all.

In our opinion, policymakers around the world, mainly between the G-7, are focusing too much effort on global rebalancing, which only encourages currency tensions, such as the current one between China and the United States. This ominously contributes to mounting protectionist sentiment and tensions. Such efforts also divert attention from the need for reforms at home. We argue that rather than focusing on global rebalancing, the G-7 nations, and to some extent the G-20, should concentrate more on repairing their domestic problems and expanding their domestic demand at the maximum sustainable rate.

We are of the position that a major rebalancing of global demand, or more explicitly, a decrease of aggregate demand in deficit countries relative to that of surplus countries must occur. This is important in order to foster smaller trade deficits and surpluses, which has already occurred during the great recession. Global demand already has undergone a major rebalancing during 2008 to 2009 as a consequence of the global credit crunch.

As depicted in Figure 6.4 countries with large current account deficits, such as the United States and Spain, also experienced the biggest housing

	US$, bn	As a percent of GDP		
	2009	2006–2008	2009	2010
United States	−378.0	−5.3	−2.9	−3.2
Spain	−74.1	−9.5	−5.4	−4.9
Italy	−71.3	−2.8	−3.4	−2.8
Australia	−40.9	−5.2	−4.1	−3.5
United Kingdom	−28.8	−2.5	−1.3	−1.7
Saudi Arabia	20.5	26.6	5.5	9.1
Russia	49.0	7.2	4.0	4.5
Japan	141.8	4.0	2.8	3.1
Germany	160.6	6.9	4.8	5.5
China	297.1	10.0	6.0	5.0

Figure 6.4 Nations with largest current account surpluses and deficits

Source: IMF, Carnegie Endowment.[6]

bubbles and have the most indebted consumers, forcing government authorities to cut much more spending than surplus countries did. For all the reasons aforementioned, we argue that a long-term trend toward rebalancing, as promoted by G-7 nations, is very unlikely to happen.

The idea may be popular among the G-7 group, but we don't believe it will gain traction among the G-20. As advanced economies, without much success so far, continue to pressure emerging markets to engage in rebalancing, the G-7, particularly the United States, may be forced to take a stand: either tackle the profound domestic vulnerabilities that have been exposed, or put at risk the open, rules-based trading system that has bolstered significant postwar prosperity.

Three Great Challenges Confronting the Global Recovery

Despite the challenges of rebalancing the global economy, we identify three great challenges confronting the global recovery. The first one is the exiting stimulus policies in the United States. The first phase of the stimulus exit, widely known as the large fiscal contraction, or "fiscal cliff," appears to have survived without significant damage to consumers and investment demands. The second phase of this stimulus exit still lies ahead in the future, when the U.S. Federal Reserve Bank begins to reduce its bond purchases. Judging by the near panic in the financial markets following a speech by Chairman Bernanke in the fall of 2013 announcing its imminence, this second phase may prove to be problematic. Yet, the U.S. Federal Reserve Bank remains sensitive to the fact that unemployment remains high as such is determined to ensure that monetary tightening will only occur in response to clear signs that the economy is strengthening.

Also, keep in mind that the dollar is the world's reserve currency, which means the United States is the only country in the world, which has no foreign trade constraint. However, this also means that the United States current account deficit needs to grow if global trade is to expand. Indeed, if the United States starts to export fewer dollars, then someone, somewhere will be unable to finance his trade. Since the United States current account deficit is the monetary base of world trade, and a reduction in the United States current account deficit is equivalent to a massive monetary tightening for the rest of the world, it is imperative to monitor the growth of central bank reserves held at the Fed. As long as these reserves continue to expand, there are few reasons to fear a hiccup in the global trade system. However, as soon as central bank reserves start to shrink, then countries around the world, emerging and advanced economies, which are running large current account deficits and large budget deficits, may find it challenging to continue to push more debt through the system. This is not true, however, in the case of China, as reserves at the Fed are contracting in real terms.

The second challenge is to avoid the sharp slowdown in emerging markets in the past couple years (2012 through 2013), particularly in China, from collapsing. Growth has slowed precipitously in the BRICS and ASEAN, among others. Yet, even with this slowdown, we believe emerging markets as a group will continue to benefit from technological advancements, high savings rates, significant investments in education, and favorable demographics, including an ever increasing middle-class. Despite the global crisis, emerging markets are still growing at an average rate of five percent. China suffers from overly large and misallocated credit-fueled investments as well as inadequate demand by households. As its huge reservoir of surplus labor depletes, China's wages are now rising fast, pointing to a country less competitive in international markets and more inclined to consume. China is unlikely to return to the fiery 9 to 10 percent growth of the last three decades, but its solid fiscal position, robust household balance sheets, and huge reserves suggest it will find a way to sustain a more moderate pace and continue to support the global recovery.

The third and greatest challenge is to complete the extremely painful adjustment of the EU's periphery. Europe's huge deviation in costs between the core countries and the periphery is significant, as discussed earlier. In fact, for the past decade, costs between Germany and some of the peripheral countries have deviated by anywhere from 20 to 40 percent. This divergence has made the peripheral economies lose competitive advantage, and has resulted in the massive trade imbalances within EU as a whole. Countries such as Portugal, Greece, Spain, and Italy need to regain international competitiveness and reorient their economy away from domestic activity, such as construction and public services, and more toward exports and import-substitutes, such as manufacturing and tourism. This is now happening at a steady if unimpressive speed and is reflected in sharply lower current account deficits. For instance, in 2012 and 2013, exports in Italy and Spain grew in line with world trade (around 2.5 to 3 percent), while imports fell about 3 times faster than GDP.

In sum, how should global trade imbalances rebalance? The inexorably deleveraging of current large trade deficits has been damaging and requires global cooperation to put into place a credible fiscal plan to bring down deficits deliberately. Such alternative solutions as monetary policy alone will continue to prove insufficient, and seeking a solution by waging a trade war should be resisted. Following such quick-fix paths could produce severe consequences for the global economy, and heavily trade-dependent countries would feel the impact even more harshly.

The best resolution, and the one Keynes urged without success on the United States in the 1920s and 1930s, is that Germany take steps to reverse its trade surplus. It could boost disposable household income and household consumption by cutting income and consumption taxes, and as German household income grows relative to the country's total production, the national savings rate automatically would drop and the trade surplus contract and eventually become a deficit. Or Germany could engineer a massive increase in infrastructure spending.

The Importance of Multilateral Global Trade

Multilateralism refers to collective, cooperative action by states—when necessary, in concert with nonstate actors—to deal with common problems and challenges when these are best managed collaboratively at the international level. Areas such as maintaining international peace and security, economic development and international trade, human rights, functional and technical cooperation, and the protection of the environment, and sustainability of resources require joint action to reduce costs and bring order and regularity to international relations. Such problems cannot be addressed unilaterally with optimum effectiveness. This rationale persists because all states, as well as some nonstate actors, face mutual vulnerabilities and intensifying interdependence. They will benefit from and are thus required to support global public goods. Even the most powerful states cannot achieve security nor maintain prosperity and health as effectively acting unilaterally or in isolation. We have seen this demonstrated again and again, and so the international system rests on a network of treaties, regimes, and international organizations and shared practices that embody common expectations, reciprocity, and equivalence of benefits.

In an interdependent, globalized, and networked world, multilateral trade will be the key aspect of international trade relations. All global trade partners depend upon multilateral agreements and the underwriting of regularity and public goods in the international trade system. But if they are to remain viable, multinational corporations (and governments), the values of multilateralism embedded in them must be reconstituted in line with 21st century principles of governance and legitimacy. Just as importantly, they must be capable of addressing contemporary challenges effectively. This may involve moving beyond the original roots of multilateral global trade, reassessing the values on which multilateral trade is based and promoted, and recognizing that contemporary and prospective challenges call for more agility, nimbleness, flexibility, adaptability, and anticipatory rather than always reactive solutions.

That said, without continual structural and procedural trading reforms, the legitimacy and performance global trading deficits will accumulate and there will be an intensifying crisis of confidence in the world's system of organized multilateral trade centered on the UN and the WTO. The values and institutions of formalized multilateral trade as currently constituted are neither optimally effective nor legitimate. The chief multilateral organizations do not meet current standards of representivity, consent, juridical accountability, rule of law, broad participation, and transparency—and therefore political legitimacy. The African continent, for the most part, is practically excluded from it, to the advantage of Sino-African multilateral trade and the peril of the West. This is an acute problem precisely because international trade organizations play an increasingly important and intrusive role in people's lives. The more this happens, the more people will realize that multilateral trade is value-laden, connoting fundamental social and political choices regarding the balance between the market and equity, human rights, governance, and democracy. Protectionism has no place in the global rebalancing of trade.

The world has become very interdependent in areas as diverse as financial markets, infectious diseases, climate change, terrorism, nuclear peace and safety, product safety, food supply and water tables, fish stocks, and ecosystem resources. In addition to their potential for provoking interstate military conflicts, these are all drivers of human insecurity because of the threat they pose to individual lives and welfare. The challenge for international trade and global governance—governance for the world to produce order, stability, and predictability even in the absence of a world government—is great, and can be broken up into six categories:

1. The evolution of international trading organizations to facilitate robust global trade responses lags behind the emergence of collective action problems such as infrastructure in emerging markets, liquidity, governance, lack of foreign direct investments, and the curbing of rampant corruption in frontier markets

2. The most pressing problems—nuclear weapons, terrorism, pandemics, food, water and fuel scarcity, climate change, and agricultural trade—are global in scope and require global solutions. These problems are major barriers to international trade, yet, the policy authority and legal capacity for coercive mobilization of the required resources for tackling them remain vested in states, mainly the West and a few markets in the East.

3. There is a disconnect between the distribution of decision-making authority in international trade institutions, such as the International Chamber of Commerce (ICC), and the distribution of military, diplomatic, and economic power in the real world. Such gap only contributes to civil chaos, which is an impediment to trade, in countries such as Sudan, Congo, Sierra Leon, and even the Delta region of Nigeria, to name a few.

4. There is also a disconnect between the concentration of decision-making authority in intergovernmental forums and the diffusion of decision-shaping influence among nonstate actors like international markets, multinationals, and civil society actors.

5. There is a mutually undermining gap between legitimacy and efficiency. Precisely what made the G-8 summits unique and valuable—informal meetings between a small number of the world's most

powerful government leaders behind closed doors on a first name basis, without intermediaries and with no notes being taken—is what provoked charges of hegemonism, secrecy, opaqueness, and lack of representation and legitimacy. The very feature that gives the UN its unique legitimacy, universal membership, makes it an inefficient body for making, implementing, and enforcing collective decisions

6. During the Cold War, the main axis around which world trade and political affairs rotated was East–West. Today this has morphed into a North–South axis. For instance, the Copenhagen conference on climate change was suboptimal in outcome in part because of the colliding worldviews of the global North and South.

The net result of these six global trading governance deficits is to disempower, disable, and incapacitate joint decision making for solving collective action problems. As a corollary, the fundamental challenge for the international community is how to restructure and reform the UN in order to reposition it at the center of collective efforts to manage current and anticipated global trading problems over the next quarter and half century.

The paradigmatic institutions of global governance have been the G-8 and the UN. The G-6/7/8, set up in 1975, was always a narrow club of *self-selected countries* and, as such, *never possessed either electoral or representative legitimacy*. Conversely, its many real global trading accomplishments notwithstanding, the UN has struggled to be relevant and effective. Both the G-8 and the UN Security Council had become structurally obsolete by the turn of the century. Looking at the two together, unlike China, Brazil, and India are not permanent members of the UN Security Council. Unlike Japan, China and India are not members of the G-8. It is difficult to imagine any real contemporary global trading, or rebalancing in this case, problem that can be addressed with the requisite degree of effectiveness and legitimacy without the active participation of all three Asian giants at the top table of decision making.

The emergence of the G-20 spoke powerfully to the need for an alternative global steering group to draw in all the world's powerful actors as responsible managers of the world order as stakeholders, not merely rule-takers. Potentially, the G-20 offered the best crossover point between legitimacy, efficiency, and effectiveness. Its purpose would be to steer policy consensus and coordination, and to mobilize the requisite political will to drive global trade reforms and address global geopolitical challenges while navigating the shifting global currents of power, wealth, and influence. But in order to be legitimate, it still must work with and not independently of or against the UN.

Unfortunately, what began as a major institutional innovation with the first G-20 leaders' summit in 2008 has fallen victim to aimless meandering and a rhetoric-action gap where photo opportunities have displaced global leadership. The group's identity has been diluted and its effectiveness compromised. Far from being a streamlined executive body for global governance, the G-20 is arguably already bloated and unwieldy.

For many, as argued by Ramesh Thakur,* "globalization is both desirable and irreversible for having underwritten a rising standard of living and material prosperity throughout the world for several decades. For some, however, globalization is the soft underbelly of corporate imperialism that plunders and profiteers on the back of rampant consumerism and almost brought the world to its knees in 2008 to 2009."[7]

There is growing divergence in income levels between countries and peoples around the world. The deepening of poverty and inequality—prosperity for a few countries and some people, marginalization and exclusion for many—has implications for social and political stability among and within states. The rapid growth of global markets has not been accompanied by the parallel development of social and economic

---

* Ramesh Thakur is Professor of International Relations and Foundation Director of the Centre for Nuclear Nonproliferation and Disarmament at the Australian National University in Canberra. He was formerly the Senior Vice Rector of the United Nations University in charge of its Peace and Governance Program at the rank of Assistant Secretary-General; Senior Adviser and Principal Writer of the UN Secretary-General's 2002 reform report; and a member of the International Commission on Intervention and State Sovereignty and one of the principal authors of its report The Responsibility to Protect. He has held full-time teaching positions in New Zealand, Australia, and Canada and serves on the advisory boards of several research institutes in Africa, Asia, Europe, and North America.

institutions to ensure balanced, inclusive, and sustainable growth. Labor rights have been less sedulously protected than capital and property rights, and global rules on trade and finance are less than equitable.

For Thakur,

> even before the global financial crisis of 2008, many emerging economies were worried about the adverse impact of globalization on economic sovereignty, cultural integrity, and social stability. "Interdependence" among unequals is tantamount to the dependence of some on international markets that function under the dominance of others. The financial crisis confirmed that absent effective regulatory institutions, rampant transnational forces could overwhelm markets, states, and civil society. It also raised questions of the roles of international financial institutions and ratings agencies—with their known proclivity to insist on austerity and reduced spending for cutting deficits instead of looking to fostering economic growth as the means to raise public revenues—in dictating policy to elected governments.[8]

Globalization has also let loose the forces of "uncivil society" and accelerated the transnational flows of terrorism, human and drug trafficking, organized crime, piracy, and pandemic diseases. The notion that endless liberalization, deregulation, and relaxation of capital and border controls (except for labor) will assure perpetual self-sustaining growth and prosperity has proven to be delusional. For developing countries, lowering all barriers to the tides of the global economy may end up drowning much of local production. But raising barriers too high may be futile or counterproductive. Where lies the golden middle?

About the Authors

Marcus Goncalves EdD, is an international management consultant with more than 25 years of experience in the United States, Latin America, Europe, Middle East, and Asia. Mr. Goncalves is the former CTO of Virtual Access Networks, which under his leadership was awarded the *Best Enterprise Product* at Comdex Fall 2001, leading to the acquisition of the company by Symantec. He holds a master's degree in Computer Information Systems and a doctorate in Educational Leadership from Boston University. He has more than 45 books published in the United States, many translated into Portuguese, German, Chinese, Korean, Japanese, and Spanish. He's often invited to speak on international business, global trade, international management, and organizational development subjects worldwide. Marcus has been lecturing at Boston University and Brandeis University for the past 11 years. He has also been a visiting professor and graduate research adviser and examiner at Saint Joseph University, in Macao, China for the past three years. He is an Associate Professor of Management, and the International Business Program Chair at Nichols College, in Dudley, MA. Dr. Goncalves can be contacted via e-mail at marcus.goncalves@nichols.edu or at marcusg@mgcgusa.com.

Harry Xia, DBA, is an Assistant Professor of Finance at the Faculty of Administration and Leadership of the University of Saint Joseph (USJ) in Macau, China. He held key management positions in finance and marketing for multinational corporations in the United States and Asia Pacific for almost 20 years before joining USJ, and still serves as an active business consultant and advisor to companies in China and its surrounding areas. His major research interests include corporate finance, international business, and corporate governance. His research has been published in journals and conference proceedings, such as *The International Review of Business Research Papers*, and presented in the Asian Business Research

Conference and Academy of International Business Annual Meeting. He holds a Doctor of Business Administration from the Hong Kong Polytechnic University and a Master of Hospitality Management from the University of Houston in Texas.

Advance Quotes for
Comparing Emerging and Advanced Markets

Goncalves and Xia provide an excellent analysis and framework for understanding the impact emerging economies will have on the global economy. Great primer for those interested in understanding the opportunities and complexities arising from the emerging markets such as CIVETS and ASEAN and their influence on the advanced economies. I highly recommend this book to anyone looking to learn more about the interplay between emerging and advanced economies and what that means for political economic shifts in the global order.

—Shaun Rein, Founder, China Market Research Group, Shanghai, China; author The End of Copycat China: The Rise of Creativity, Innovation and Individualism in Asia

This material accurately describes the economic realities outside the American sandbox. From state-sponsored inflationary policy to the global transfer of wealth, it is all here. A must read for any executive who performs asset management and business operations on the world scene.

—Jim Willey, PE; Director Pearl Energy Philippines Operating Inc, Philippines

A lucid, compact, and robust description and analysis about current global economic trends, which I enjoyed reading. I've learned quite a lot about the forces and fields that are trying to emerge, survive, and thrive in an age of perennial complexity, black swans, and wicked fuzzy situations we and the next generations will have to tackle.

—Fabian Szulanski, Director, System Dynamics Center. Director, Learning Lab. ITBA, Instituto Tecnologico de Buenos Aires, Argentina

Forget the repeated crises of the 1980s and 1990s. The true threat now comes from the developed world (advanced markets), with dodgy politics, weak economies, and an enormous debt overhang. It is not just that the west is lost. Emerging markets have also improved immeasurably since the fall of the Berlin Wall, as Soviet and U.S. interference reduced and democracy took hold in many places. Electorates at the emerging markets are willing to take short-term pain for long-term stability, while monetary policy is far better run. Local institutional investors now play a big part in many emerging markets, contributing to that stability. Curious to know more? Like I did, you must read *Comparing Emerging and Advanced Markets.*

> —*Alexandre Mesquita, MSc, Member of the Executive Board at DNA Hunter and Strategy, and Business Development Director at New Space Group, São Paulo, SP, Brazil*

The hospitality industry is a major global industry in terms of GDP. *Comparing Advanced and Emerging Markets,* underlines the growth opportunities and the risks the hotel business is exposed to. This book makes for mandatory reading for major hotel developers and operators, especially in emerging markets.

> —*Gert Noordzy, International Hotelier and Hotel Opening Expert, Macau S.A.R, China*

It is often forgotten that Adam Smith, known as the father of Economics, was himself a professor of Moral Philosophy. Rather than elaborate pious abstractions, he chose to delve into the complex details of the exchange of value that governs so much of men's lives. Here surely were the nodes of our ethical life. But, more he found that the systems themselves bore justice, fairness and equality or the contrary. Hence the name of his book, *The Wealth of Nations.* It is from this perspective that one may appreciate Goncalves and Xia's book. Not a technical economics tome, but one that illuminates the systems under which we now live. Understanding is the first step to changing systems for greater justice, fairness and equality.

> —*Jose Cardoso, Director of Education Programs, Pacific Oaks College, California, USA*

Goncalves and Xia map out the financial past, present, and future of emerging markets and their influence on the global economy. Providing historical facts, quantitative data, and an analysis of current trends, this book includes thoughts and contributions from scholars, the banking industry, and the media, and serves as a useful reference on the economic and fiscal forces being played around the world. Filled with all the disruptive elements of scholarly review, it invites us to reflect upon certain assumptions, urges us to stay alert, and to consider how we might, as citizens of the world, contribute to a sustainable balance between the world economies. Written by non-economists, the presentation and observations are refreshing and informative for all levels of readership.

—Yvette Jusseaume, Assistant Director, Alliance—a partnership between Columbia University, Ecole Polytechnique, Sciences Po and Paris 1 Panthéon-Sorbonne, USA

At this time of unprecedented change, I felt my understanding of the economies, politics, and condition of our global landscape was meager at best. *Comparing Advanced and Emerging Markets* is a welcome contribution providing a practical working knowledge of the great shift powered by the emerging markets and the disruption of so many economies at war. Comprehending this game-changing crisis provides the knowledge that many of us require in order to make decisions where uncertainty is often an overriding variable.

—Kerri Holt, Special Projects Officer, Dallas Independent School District, USA

This is compulsive reading for those who are interested in understanding the nature of the global financial system in 21st century and the emergent influences driving it. Erudite and accessible this book articulates the tensions underlining the global geopolitical systems and proposes ways of thinking about how the risks underlying these systems need to be understood so as not to affect global economic stability. Well researched and thought provoking!

—Dr Ralph Kerle, Global Strategic Growth and Innovation Specialist, Sydney, Australia

This is a must-read book for those wishing to improve their understanding of how advanced economies and emerging markets interact across the globe in current times. The rigorous analysis and innovative insight provide us with a powerful tool to perceive the undergoing rebalance of global trade.

—Filipe Manuel Peixoto Pereira, Senior Legal Advisor at Law Reform and International Law Bureau, Macau SAR Government

Notes

Chapter 1

1. Macleans (2010)
2. CNN (2009).
3. G20 (2013). (Last accessed in October 3, 2013).
4. IMF (2013).
5. Business Insider (2013).
6. China The People's Daily (2011).
7. Bremmer (2013).
8. Orgaz, Molina, and Carrasco (2011).
9. Mobiot (2013).
10. Project leader, Joseph Francois, research accessed on October 06, 2013, http://trade.ec.europa.eu/doclib/docs/2013/march/tradoc_150737.pdf
11. Burnett (2013).
12. American Manufacturing (2013).
13. Public Citizen (2013).
14. Reinhart and Sbrancia (2011).
15. McKinnon (1973).
16. Rickards (2011).

Chapter 2

1. IMF (October, 2013).
2. *Forbes* (2000).
3. *Forbes* (2007).
4. Wilson and Purushothaman (2003).
5. Hawksworth (2008).
6. Poncet (2006).
7. OECD (n.d.)
8. ASEAN (2014).
9. Cheewatrakoolpong, Sabhasri, and Bunditwattanawong (2013), IDBI, # 409.
10. Investvine (October 2013).
11. IHS (2009)
12. Durand, Madaschi, and Terribile (1998), No. 195.
13. Krugman (1996).
14. Kowitt (2009).

15. Reuters (2011).
16. SouthAfrica.info (June 2012).
17. Foroohar (2009).
18. Investopedia (2008).
19. O'Neill (2011).
20. Foroohar (2009).
21. Young (2006).
22. Haub (2012).
23. Faulconbridge (2008).
24. Mortished (2008).
25. Halpin (2009).
26. SIPA.Columbia (n.d.)
27. Dresen (2011).
28. The Economist (2009).
29. The Economist (2009).
30. O'Neill (2005), No. 134.
31. WorldBank (n.d.).
32. Wiley Online Library (2013).
33. IMF Reports (2013), Middle East and North Africa: Defining the Road Ahead, Regional Economic Outlook Update, Middle East and Central Asia Department.
34. Saseendran (2013).
35. IMF (November 2013).
36. QNB Group (2013).

Chapter 3

1. Schwartz (2013).
2. Blanchart (2013).
3. HeritageFoundation (n.d.).
4. Golf, Boccia, and Fleming (2012).
5. Rand (1957).
6. Golf, Boccia, and Fleming (2013).
8. OECD (2013).
8. IndexMundi (2011).
9. Matsui (2012).
10. Wheatley (2013).
11. Taborda (2013).
12. Papademos (2006).

13. Freeman (2006).
14. Pain, Koske, and Sollie (2006).
15. IMF (2013).
16. O'Neill (2012).
17. BusinessInsider (August 2012).
18. HappyPlanetIndex (n.d.).

Chapter 4

1. Wagstyl (2013).
2. The Economist's Writers (2013).
3. Amadeo (2013).
4. Rodrik (2009).
5. IMF (2010).
6. Svensson (2008).
7. Jahan (2012).
8. The Economist (November 2013).
9. Gulf Times (December 2013).
10. Hood (2013).
11. The Economist (January 2012).
12. Williams (1983).
13. Johnson (2000).
14. Bukharin (1915 [1972]).
15. Schmidt (November 2003).
16. The Economist (January 2012).
17. The Economist (January 2012).
18. Bremmer (July 2009).
19. Das (2013).
20. The Economist (2013).
21. The Economist (2013).

Chapter 5

1. The Economist (2013).
2. TradingEconomics (September 2013).
3. Guerrera (2013).
4. Mises (May 2012).
5. The Telegraph Staff Writers (2013).

Chapter 6

1. Huang (2013).
2. CFAInstitute (November 2013).
3. Investopedia (November 2013).
4. Caballero (2009).
5. Pettis (2013).
6. CarnegieEndowment (November 2013).
7. Newman, Thakur, and Tirman (2006), Eds.
8. Heine and Thakur (2011), Eds.

References

Abulof, U. 2011. "What Is the Arab Third Estate?" *Huffington Post*. http://www. huffingtonpost.com/uriel-abulof/what-is-the-arab-third-es_b_832628.html, (11/12/2013).

Afrol News of Morocco Staff Writers. 2011. "Morocco King on holiday as people consider revolt," *Afrol News*. http://www.afrol.com/articles/37175, (11/01/2013).

Afrol News Staff Writers. 2011. "New clashes in occupied Western Sahara," *Afrol News*. http://www.afrol.com/articles/37450, (10/25/2013).

Ahmed, M. 2010. "Trade Competitiveness and Growth MENA," *World Economic Forum's Arab World Competitiveness Review*. http://www.imf.org/external/np/vc/2010/103010.htm, (01/03/2014).

Akhtar, S.I.; M.J. Bolle; and R.M. Nelson. 2013. "U.S. Trade and Investment in the Middle East and North Africa: Overview and Issues for Congress," *Congress Research Service*. http://fpc.state.gov/documents/organization/206138.pdf.

Al Jazeera Staff Writers. 2011. "Sudan police clash with protesters," *Al Jazeera*. http://www.aljazeera.com/news/africa/2011/01/2011130131451294670.html, (09/12/2013).

Al Jazeera Staff Writers. 2011. "Tunisia's Ben Ali flees amid unrest," *Al Jazeera*. http://www.aljazeera.com/news/africa/2011/01/20111153616298850.html, (11/15/2013).

Al Masah Capital Management Limited. 2010. "China and India's Growing Influence in the MENA Region: Their Legacy and Future Footprint." http://s3.amazonaws.com/zanran_storage/ae.zawya.com/ContentPages/142996358.pdf, (on 01/03/2014).

Al-Ansary, K. 2011. "Iraq's Sadr followers march against Bahrain crackdown," *Reuters*. http://www.reuters.com/article/2011/03/16/us-bahrain-iraq-idUSTRE72F4U220110316, (11/12/2013).

Aljazeera Staff Writers. 2011. "Thousands protest in Jordan," *Al Jazeera*. http://www.aljazeera.com/news/middleeast/2011/01/2011128125157509196.html, (10/25/2013).

Alternative Economic System. Al Jazeera Center for Studies. Retrieved from http://studies.aljazeera.net/en/reports/2013/06/20136474134190632.html, (12/19/2013).

Alternative Economic System. Al Jazeera Center for Studies. Retrieved from http://studies.aljazeera.net/en/reports/2013/06/20136474134190632.html.

Amadeo, K. 2013. "What Is a Currency War?" http://useconomy.about.com/od/tradepolicy/g/Currency-Wars.htm.

Sen, A. 1999. *Development as Freedom*. Oxford, United Kingdom: Oxford University Press.

Ambrose, S. and D. Brinkley. 2011. *Rise to Globalism*. New York, NY: Penguin Group.

American Chamber of Commerce, International Affairs. 2013. "ASEAN Business Outlook Survey," *Singapore Business Federation*. http://www.amcham.org.sg/wp-content/uploads/2013/08/2014ABOS.pdf, (10/24/2013).

Amin, M. 2009. "Labor Regulation and Employment in India's Retail Stores," *Journal of Comparative Economics* 37 (1): 47–61.

Arabia Monitor. 2012. "Shifting Sands, Shifting Trade: Building a New Silk Route," *Middle East and North Africa Outlook Q4 2012*. http://www.researchandmarkets.com/reports/2253210/q4_2012_mena_outlook_shifting_sands_shifting, (12/19/2013).

Arkalgud, A.P. 2011. "Filling "institutional voids" in emerging markets," *Forbes*. http://www.forbes.com/sites/infosys/2011/09/20/filling-institutional-voids-in-emerging-markets/

Asian Development Bank. 2013. "Asian Development Outlook 2013 Update," *ADB*. Manila, http://www.adb.org/countries/pakistan/economy, (12/20/2013).

Associate Press Staff Writers. 2011. "Algeria protest draws thousands," *CBC News World/Associate Press*. http://www.cbc.ca/news/world/algeria-protest-draws-thousands-1.1065078, (11/02/2013).

Bain & Company's Staff Analysts. 2012. "A world awash in money," *Bain & Company*. http://www.bain.com/publications/articles/a-world-awash-in-money.aspx, (12/07/2013).

Bakri, N. and D. Goodman. 2011. "Thousands in Yemen Protest against the Government," *The New York Times*. http://www.nytimes.com/2011/01/28/world/middleeast/28yemen.html?_r=0, (11/11/2013).

Barrera, C. and T. Dobbyn. 2012. "U.S. says BizJet settles foreign bribery charges," *Reuters*. http://www.reuters.com/article/2012/03/14/us-mexico-lufthansa-idUSBRE82D1H220120314, (10/28/2013).

Barstow, D. 2012. "Vast Mexican Bribery Case Hushed Up by Wal-Mart After High-Level Struggle," *The New York Times*. http://www.nytimes.com/2012/04/22/business/at-wal-mart-in-mexico-a-bribe-inquiry-silenced.html?_r=0, (05/13/2012).

BBC News Middle East Staff Writers. 2011. "Man dies after setting himself on fire in Saudi Arabia," *BBC News*. http://www.bbc.co.uk/news/world-middle-east-12260465, (11/04/2013).

BBC News Staff Writers. 2011. "News Corp shares hit two-year low on hacking arrest," *BBC World News*. http://www.bbc.co.uk/news/business-14181119, (02/04/2012).

Bhattacharya, R. and H. Wolde. 2010a. "Constraints on Growth in the MENA Region," *IMF Working Papers*, 1–21.

Bhattacharya, R. and H. Wolde. 2010b. "Constraints on Trade in the MENA Region," *IMF Working Papers*, 1–18.

Bishku, M. B. 2010. "South Africa and the Middle East," *Journal Essay Middle East Policy Council*. Fall 2010, Volume XVII, Number 3.

Blanchart, O. 2013. "Advanced Economies Strengthening, Emerging Market Economies Weakening," *iMFDirect*. http://blog-imfdirect.imf.org/2013/10/08/advanced-economies-strengthening-emerging-market-economies-weakening/, (10/15/2013).

Blanke, J. 2013. "The Global Competitiveness Report 2013-2014," *World Economic Forum*. http://www.weforum.org/issues/global-competitiveness, (11/24/2013).

Bonham, C.; B. Gangnes; and A.V. Assche. 2004. "Fragmentation and East Asia's Information Technology Trade," *Department of Economics at the University of Hawaii at Manoa, and University of California at Davis*. Working Paper No. 04.09. http://www.economics.hawaii.edu/research/workingpapers/WP_04-9.pdf, (12/01/2013).

Boone, Elisabeth. 2007. "Political Risk in Emerging Markets," *The Rough Notes Company, Inc.* http://www.roughnotes.com/rnmagazine/2007/october 07/10p060.htm, (Last accessed Nov. 11, 2013).

Brahmbhatt, M.; O. Canuto; and S. Ghosh. 2010. "Currency Wars Yesterday and Today." *Economic Premise*, 43.

Bremmer, I. 2009. *State capitalism and the crisis*. Eurasia Group.

Bremmer, I. 2013. *Every Nation for Itself: Winners and Losers in a G-zero World*. Portfolio/Penguin, New York City, NY.

Bukharin, N. 1972. *Imperialism and World Economy*. London: Merlin.

Burnett, B. 2013. "5 Problems With the Trans Pacific Partnership," Huff Post, http://www.huffingtonpost.com/bob-burnett/trans-pacific-partnership_b_4479420.html, (05/12/2014).

Business Standard of India Staff Writers. 2011. "BRICS is passé, time now for 3G:Citi," *Business Standard*. New Delhi, India. http://www.business-standard.com/india/news/brics-is-passe-time-now-for- percent5C3g percent5C-citi/126725/on, (11/01/2013).

Caballero, R. 2009. "Sudden Financial Arrest." *10th Jacques Polak Annual Research Conference*. http://www.imf.org/external/np/res/seminars/2009/arc/pdf/caballero.pdf, (11/30/2013).

Cammett, M. 2013. "Development and Underdevelopment in the Middle East and North Africa." In Carol Lancaster and Nicolas van de Walle (eds.), *Handbook of the Politics of Development*. New York: Oxford University Press, 2013 (Forthcoming). Available at SSRN: http://ssrn.com/abstract=2349387, (12/20/2013).

Canuto, O. 2010. "Toward a Switchover of Locomotives in the Global Economy." *Economic Premise*, 33.

Canuto, O., and M. Giugale (Eds.). 2010. *The day after tomorrow — A handbook on the future of economic policy in the developing world*. Washington, DC: World Bank.

Cartas, J. 2010. "Dollarization Declines in Latin America, Finance and Development," March 2010, Volume 47, No. 1. http://www.imf.org/external/pubs/ft/fandd/2010/03/pdf/spot.pdf, (11/05/2013).

Cashin, P.; M.K. Mohaddes; and M.M. Raissi. 2012. "The Global Impact of the Systemic Economies and MENA," *Business Cycles* (Working Paper No. 12-255). International Monetary Fund.

Cavusgil, S. T. 1997. "Measuring The Potential of Emerging Markets: An Indexing Approach," *Business Horizons*. January-February 1997, Vol. 40 Number 1, 87–91.

Cavusgil, S.T.; T. Kiyak; and S. Yeniyurt. 2004. "Complementary Approaches to Preliminary Foreign Market Opportunity Assessment: Country Clustering and Country Ranking," *Industrial Marketing Management*, October 2004, Volume 33, Issue 7, 607–617.

Central Intelligence Agency. 2013. "The World Factbook," https://www.cia.gov/library/publications/the-world-factbook/, (09/23/13).

Cheema, F. 2004. "Macroeconomic Stability of Pakistan: The Role of the IMF and World Bank (1997–2003)," *Programme in Arms Control, Disarmament, and International Security (ACDIS)*. University of Illinois at Urbana-Champaign. http://acdis.illinois.edu/assets/docs/250/MacroeconomicStabilityofPakistanTheRoleoftheIMFandWorldBank19972003.pdf, (12/14/2013).

Cheewatrakoolpong, K.; C. Sabhasri; and N. Bunditwattanawong. 2013. "Impact of the ASEAN Economic Community on ASEAN Production Networks," *IDBI*, #409. http://www.adbi.org/files/2013.02.21.wp409.impact.asean.production.networks.pdf, (03/12/2013).

Chheang, V. 2008. "The Political Economy of Tourism in Cambodia," *Asia Pacific Journal of Tourism Research* 13 (3): 281–297.

The People's Daily. 2011. "Asia to play bigger role on world stage, G20: ADB report." *The People's Daily*. April 26, 2011. http://english.people.com.cn/90001/90778/98506/7361425.html, (October 1, 2013).

Clinton, H. 2011. "America's Pacific Century," *Foreign Policy*. http://www.foreignpolicy.com/articles/2011/10/11/americas_pacific_century, (11/12/2012).

Colombo, J. 2013. "Why The Worst Is Yet To Come For Indonesia's Epic Bubble Economy," *Forbes*. http://www.forbes.com/sites/jessecolombo/2013/10/03/why-the-worst-is-yet-to-come-for-indonesias-epic-bubble-economy/2/, (10/05/2013).

Condon, S. 2013. "Obama appeals to senators to hold off on more Iran sanctions," *CBSNews*. http://www.cbsnews.com/news/obama-appeals-to-senators-to-hold-off-on-more-iran-sanctions/, (12/19/2013).

Corrigan, T. 2007 "Mauritania: Country Made Slavery Illegal Last Month," *The East African Standard*. http://www.saiia.org.za/opinion-analysis/mauritania-made-slavery-illegal-last-month, (11/10/2013).

Crawford, D. and D. Searcey. 2010. "U.S. Joins H-P Bribery Investigation". *The Wall Street Journal*. http://online.wsj.com/news/articles/SB100014240527023046287045751861511155576646, (12/28/2012).

Daniele, V. and U. Marani. 2006. "Do institutions matter for FDI? A comparative analysis for the MENA countries." *University Library*, Munich, Germany.

Das, S. 2013. "The New Economic Nationalism," *ABC Australia*. http://www.abc.net.au/news/2013-09-30/das-the-new-economic-nationalism/4988690, (12/12/2013).

Deen, E.S. 2013. BRICS & Egypt: An Opportunity to Begin Creating

Mutum, D.S.; S.K. Roy; and E. Kipnis (eds). 2014. *Marketing Cases from Emerging Markets*. New York: Springer.

Donnison, J. 2011. "Palestinians Emboldened by Arab Spring," *Ramallah: BBC News*. http://www.bbc.co.uk/news/world-middle-east-13417788, (11/16/2013).

Dresen, F.J. 2011. "BRICS: Shaping the New Global Architecture," *Woodrow Wilson International Center for Scholars*. http://www.wilsoncenter.org/publication/brics-shaping-the-new-global-architecture, (4/5/2012).

Durand, M.; C. Madaschi; and F. Terribile. 1998. "Trends in OECD Countries' International Competitiveness: The Influence of Emerging Market Economies," *OECD Economics Department Working Paper, No. 195*.

Economists Staff Writers. 2010. "BRICS and BICIS." *The Economist*. http://www.economist.com/blogs/theworldin2010/2009/11/acronyms_4, (11/9/2012).

Economists Staff Writers. 2012. "And the winner is...," *The Economist*. http://www.economist.com/node/21542926, (12/13/2013).

Economists Staff Writers. 2012. "Pros and Cons: Mixed Bags," *The Economist*. http://www.economist.com/node/21542929, (12/13/2013).

Economists Staff Writers. 2013. "Taking Europe's Pulse," *The Economist*. http://www.economist.com/blogs/graphicdetail/2013/11/european-economy-guide, (12/13/2013).

Economists Staff Writers. 2013. "When Giants Slow Down," *The Economist*. http://www.economist.com/news/briefing/21582257-most-dramatic-

and-disruptive-period-emerging-market-growth-world-has-ever-seen, (12/13/2013).

Economists Staff Writers. 2012. "The Rise of State Capitalism," *The Economist*. http://www.economist.com/node/21543160, (12/13/2013).

Economists Staff Writers. 2013. "It's the Politics, Stupid," *The Economist*. http://www.economist.com/news/leaders/21574495-economy-faces-collapse-broader-based-government-needed-take-tough-decisions-its, (11/12/2013).

Economists Staff Writers. (2013). "The Gated Globe," *The Economist*. http://www.economist.com/news/special-report/21587384-forward-march-globalisation-has-paused-financial-crisis-giving-way, (11/12/2013).

Economists Staff Writers. 2013. "The Perils of Falling Inflation," *The Economist*. http://www.economist.com/news/leaders/21589424-both-america-and-europe-central-bankers-should-be-pushing-prices-upwards-perils-falling, (11/12/2013).

Economists Staff Writers. 2012. "Gushers and Guns," *The Economist*. http://www.economist.com/node/21550304, (12/11/2013).

The Economist's Writers. (2013). When giants slow down. The Economist, 07/27/2013. http://www.economist.com/news/briefing/21582257-most-dramatic-and-disruptive-period-emerging-market-growth-world-has-ever-seen. (last accessed on 08/15/2014).

Newman, E.; R. Thakur, and J. Tirman (eds). 2006. *Multilateralism Under Challenge? Power, International Order, and Structural Change*. Tokyo: United Nations University Press.

Embassy of Colombia in Washington D.C. 2013. *About Colombia*. http://www.colombiaemb.org/overview, (10/30/2013).

Ernst & Young and Oxford Economics. 2011. *Trading Places: The Emergence of New Patterns of International Trade. Growing Beyond Series*. Ernst Young & Oxford Economics.

Evans-Pritchard, Ambrose. 2013. "IMF Sours on BRICs and Doubts Eurozone Recovery Claims," *The Telegraph*. http://www.telegraph.co.uk/finance/financialcrisis/10365206/IMF-sours-on-BRICs-and-doubts-eurozone-recovery-claims.html, (11/08/2013).

Faulconbridge, G. 2008. "BRICs Helped by Western Finance Crisis: Goldman," *Reuters*. http://www.reuters.com/article/2008/06/08/us-russia-forum-bric-idUSL071126420080608, (07/12/2012).

Foroohar, R. 2009. "BRICs Overtake G7 By 2027," *Newsweek*. http://www.newsweek.com/brics-overtake-g7-2027-76001, (04/12/2009).

Fox News Staff Writers. 2013. "IMF Issues Warning on South African Economy," *Fox News*. http://www.foxnews.com/world/2013/10/01/imf-issues-warning-on-south-african-economy/, (10/24/2013).

Freeland, C. 2012. *Plutocrats: The Rise of the New Global Super-Rich and the Fall of Everyone Else*. New York City, NY: Penguin Press.

Freeman, R. 2006. "The Great Doubling: The Challenge of the New Global Labor Market," *European Central Bank*. http://eml.berkeley.edu/~webfac/eichengreen/e183_sp07/great_doub.pdf, 11/02/2013).

Garcia-Herrero, A. 2012. "BBVA EAGLES Emerging and Growth-Leading Economies," *BBVA Research*. http://www.bbvaresearch.com/KETD/fbin/mult/120215_BBVAEAGLES_Annual_Report_tcm348-288784.pdf?ts=1642012, (11/01/2013).

Garcia-Palafox, G. 2012. "Walmart Bribery Allegations: Watchdog Group Says Mexican Government Should Investigate Claims Of Vast Bribery Campaign," *Huffington Post*. http://www.huffingtonpost.com/2012/04/22/walmart-bribery-allegations-watchdog-urges-probe_n_1444488.html, (04/23/2012).

Geromel, R. 2013. "Forbes Top 10 Billionaire Cities - Moscow Beats New York Again," *Forbes*. http://www.forbes.com/sites/ricardogeromel/2013/03/14/forbes-top-10-billionaire-cities-moscow-beats-new-york-again/, (10/30/2013).

Ghanem, H. and S. Shaikh. 2013. "On the Brink: Preventing Economic Collapse and Promoting Inclusive Growth in Egypt and Tunisia," *Brookings*. http://www.brookings.edu/research/papers/2013/11/economic-recovery-tunisia-egypt-shaikh-ghanem, (12/12/2013).

Ghosh A.R.; M. Chamon; C. Crowe; J.I. Kim; and J.D. Ostry. 2009. "Coping with the Crisis: Policy Options for Emerging Market Countries," *International Monetary Fund*. http://www.imf.org/external/pubs/ft/spn/2009/spn0908.pdf, (12/12/2013).

GlobalEdge. 2013. "Market Potential Index (MPI) For Emerging Markets – 2013," *Michigan State University*, International Business Center. Retrieved from http://globaledge.msu.edu/mpi

Golf, E.; R. Boccia; and J. Fleming. 2012. "Federal Spending per Household Is Skyrocketing, Federal Budget in Pictures," *The Heritage Foundation*. http://www.heritage.org/federalbudget/federal-spending-per-household, (01/23/2013).

Golf, E.; R. Boccia; and J. Fleming. 2013. "2013 Index of Economic Freedom," *The Heritage Foundation*. http://www.heritage.org/index/ranking, (01/23/2013).

Grewal, K. 2010. "CIVETS: The Next Gateway to Growth," *Daily Markets*. http://www.dailymarkets.com/stock/2010/08/24/civets-the-next-gateway-to-growth/, (02/13/2011).

Gronholt-Pedersen, J. 2012. "Cambodia Aims for Offshore Production Next Year." *The Wall Street Journal*. http://online.wsj.com/news/articles/SB10000872396390443507204578020023711640726, (02/11/2013).

Guerrera, F. 2013. "Currency War Has Started." *The Wall Street Journal*. http://online.wsj.com/news/articles/SB10001424127887324761004578283684195892250, (12/13/2013).

Halpin, T. 2009. "Brazil, Russia, India and China Form Bloc to Challenge U.S. Dominance," *The Times*. http://www.timesonline.co.uk/tol/news/world/us_and_americas/article6514737.ece, (23/03/2011).

Hamburger, T.; B. Dennis; and J. L. Yang. 2012. "Wal-Mart Took Part in Lobbying Campaign to Amend Anti-Bribery Law," *The Washington Post*. http://www.washingtonpost.com/business/economy/wal-mart-took-part-in-lobbying-campaign-to-amend-anti-bribery-law/2012/04/24/gIQAyZcdfT_story_1.html, (11/19/2012).

Haub, C. 2012. "The BRIC Countries," *Population Reference Bureau*. http://www.prb.org/Publications/Articles/2012/brazil-russia-india-china.aspx, (12/05/2012).

Hauser, C. 2013. "Iraq: Maliki Demands That Protesters Stand Down," *The New York Times*. http://www.nytimes.com/2013/01/03/world/middleeast/iraq-maliki-demands-that-protesters-stand-down.html?_r=1&, (02/16/2013).

Hawksworth, J. 2011. "The World in 2005: How Big will the Major Emerging Market Economies Get and How Can the OECD Compete," *Price Waterhouse Coopers*. http://www.pwc.com/en_GX/gx/psrc/pdf/world_in_2050_carbon_emissions_psrc.pdf, (last accessed on 01/02/2011).

Hawksworth, J. and D. Chan. 2013. "World in 2050: The BRICS and Beyond: Prospects, Challenges, and Opportunities," *PWC Economics*. http://www.pwc.com/en_GX/gx/world-2050/assets/pwc-world-in-2050-report-january-2013.pdf, (03/12/2013).

Hayton, B. 2006. "Vietnam: ¿comunista o consumista?," *BBC Mundo*, Hanoi. http://news.bbc.co.uk/hi/spanish/business/newsid_5308000/5308298.stm, (07/22/2012).

Heng, D. 2011. "Managing Cambodia's economic fragility," *CamproPost*. http://campropost.org/2011/07/15/managing-cambodia-s-economic-fragility.html, (10/10/2013).

Hood, M. 2013. "The Stubborn Inflation in Emerging Markets," *Institutional Investors*. http://www.institutionalinvestor.com/gmtl/3279243/The-Stubborn-Inflation-in-Emerging-Markets.html, (11/15/2013).

Hoti, I. 2004. "Pakistan Ends Ties with IMF Tomorrow," *PakistaniDefence.com*. http://forum.pakistanidefence.com/index.php?showtopic=36120, (10/12/2013).

HSBC Bank. 2013. "India Trade Forecast Report - HSBC Global Connections," *HSBC Global Connections Report*. India. https://globalconnections.hsbc.com/global/en/tools-data/trade-forecasts/in, (12/19/2013).

Human Rights Watch Staff Writers. 2012. "Iran: Arrest Sweeps Target Arab Minority," *Human Rights Watch*. http://www.refworld.org/docid/4f34de412.html, (11/03/2013).

Hutchinson, M. 2010. "The CIVETS: Windfall Wealth From the 'New' BRIC Economies," *European Business Review.* http://www.europeanbusinessreview.eu/page.asp?pid=829, (11/02/2013).

IMF Reports. 2013. Middle East and North Africa: Defining the Road Ahead, Regional Economic Outlook Update," *Middle East and Central Asia Department.* http://www.imf.org/external/pubs/ft/reo/2013/mcd/eng/pdf/mcdreo0513.pdf., (11/02/1013).

IMF Report. 2013. "Economic Growth Moderates Across Middle East," *IMF Survey Magazine.* http://www.imf.org/external/pubs/ft/survey/so/2013/car052113a.htm, (01/03/2014).

IMF Report. 2013. *World Economic Outlook.* http://www.imf.org/external/pubs/ft/weo/2013/01/weodata/index.aspx, (04/12/2013).

IMF Report. 2010a. Global Financial Stability Report. April.

IMF Report. 2013. "South Africa Searches for Faster Growth, More Jobs," *IMF Survey Magazine.* http://www.imf.org/external/pubs/ft/survey/so/2013/car080713a.htm, (11/05/2013).

IMF Report. 2006. "Globalization and Inflation," *World Economic Outlook.* Washington D.C. http://www.imf.org/external/pubs/ft/weo/2006/01/pdf/weo0406.pdf, (11/08/2013).

IMF Report. 2013. "Transitions and Tensions," *World Economic Outlook.* http://www.imf.org/external/pubs/ft/weo/2013/02/., (11/02/2013).

International News of Pakistan Staff Writers. 2012. "Asia Nations to Double Currency Swap Deal," *Pakistan.* http://www.thenews.com.pk/Todays-News-3-98519-Briefs, (11/05/2013).

Jahan, S. 2012. "Inflation Targeting: Holding the Line," *IMF.* Washington DC.

Jeong, C.H. and N.F. Nawi. 2007. *Principles of Public Administration: An Introduction.* Kuala Lumpur: Karisma Publications.

Johnson, A. G. 2000. *The Blackwell Dictionary of Sociology.* Oxford: Blackwell Publishing.

Heine, J. and R. Thakur (Eds.). 2011. *The Dark Side of Globalization.* Tokyo: UnitedNations University Press.

Khaithu. 2012. "Traditional Market in Vietnam: A Social and Economic Angle," 10/15/2012. http://khaithu.wordpress.com/2012/10/15/traditional-market-in-vn-a-social-and-economic-angle/, (11/01/2013).

Kilpatrick, S. 2010. "Who Gets to Rule the World," MacLean's Canada News. http://www.macleans.ca/news/canada/who-gets-to-rule-the-world/, (7/1/2010).

Khanna, T., and K.G. Palepu. 2010. *Winning in Emerging Markets: A Roadmap for Strategy and Execution.* Boston, MA: Harvard Business School Publishing.

Koelbl, S. 2011. "It Will Not Stop: Syrian Uprising Continues Despite Crackdown," *Der Spiegel.* http://www.spiegel.de/international/world/it-will-not-stop-syrian-uprising-continues-despite-crackdown-a-753517.html, (11/10/2013).

Kose, M.A.; P. Loungani; and M.E. Terrones. 2012. "Tracking the Global Recovery," *IMF Finance and Development Magazine*. Vol. 49, No. 2.

Kowalczyk-Hoyer, B. and S. Côté-Freeman. 2013."Transparency in Corporate Reporting: Assessing Emerging Market Multinationals," *Transparency International.* http://transparency.org/whatwedo/pub/transparency_in_corporate_reporting_assessing_emerging_market_multinational, (11/02/2013).

Lewis, P.; A. Sen; and Z. Tabary. 2011. "New Routes to the Middle East: Perspectives on Inward Investment and Trade," *Economist Intelligence Unit.* https://www.business.hsbc.co.uk/1/PA_esf-ca-app-content/content/pdfs/en/new_routes_to_middle_east.pdf, (01/03/2014).

Lobe, J. 2013. "Scowcroft, Brzezinski Urge Iran Accord," *Lobe Log: Foreign Policy.* http://www.lobelog.com/scowcroft-brzezinski-urge-iran-accord/, (12/16/2013).

Manson, K. 2011. "Pro-Democracy Protests Reach Djibouti," *Financial Times.* http://www.ft.com/intl/cms/s/0/001f94f6-3d18-11e0-bbff-00144feabdc0.html?siteedition=intl, (10/25/2013).

Manyika, J. et al. 2012. "Manufacturing the Future: The Next Era of Global Growth and Innovation," *McKinsey Global Institute,* http://www.mckinsey.com/insights/manufacturing/the_future_of_manufacturing, (12/01/2013).

Markey, P. 2010. "Colombia's Santos Takes Office with Strong Mandate," *Reuters.com.* http://www.reuters.com/article/2010/08/07/us-colombia-santos-idUSTRE6760DD20100807, (10/30/2012).

Marquand, R. 2011. "Amid BRICS' Rise and `Arab Spring', a New Global Order Forms," *Christian Science Monitor.* http://www.csmonitor.com/World/Global-Issues/2011/1018/Amid-BRICS-rise-and-Arab-Spring-a-new-global-order-forms, (01/02/2013).

Matsui, K. 2012. "A View from Japan," *Goldman Sachs.* http://www.youtube.com/watch?v=bfkqe4vLdFY, (11/10/2013).

Maxwell, J. 2012. "Beyond the BRICS: How to Succeed in Emerging Markets (by Really Trying)," *PWC.* http://www.pwc.com/us/en/view/issue-15/succeed-emerging-markets.jhtml, (11/27/2013).

McCrummen, S. 2011. "13 Killed in Iraq's 'Day of Rage' Protests," *The Washington Post.* http://www.washingtonpost.com/wp-dyn/content/article/2011/02/24/AR2011022403117.html, (06/12/2011).

McKinnon, R. I. 1973. *Money and Capital in Economic Development.* Washington, DC: Brookings Institution Press.

Middle East Online Staff Writers. 2011. "Kuwaiti Stateless Protest for Third Day," *Middle East Online.* http://www.middle-east-online.com/english/?id=44476, (10/25/2013).

Ministry of Economy and Finance of Cambodia. 2013. "Council for the Development of Cambodia (CDC)," *Economic Trends.* http://www.

cambodiainvestment.gov.kh/investment-enviroment/economic-trend.html, (11/04/2013).

Mitchell, J. 2013. "Why Emerging Markets Are Tough to Enter," *HSBC Global Connections.* https://globalconnections.hsbc.com/canada/en/articles/why-emerging-markets-are-tough-enter, (12/16/2013).

Mobiot, G. 2013. "This Transatlantic Trade Deal Is a Full-Frontal Assault on Democracy," The Guardian, UK, http://www.theguardian.com/commentisfree/2013/nov/04/us-trade-deal-full-frontal-assault-on-democracy. (05/25/2014).

Moghadam, R. 2010. "How Did Emerging Markets Cope in the Crisis?, the Strategy, Policy, and Review Department, in consultation with other IMF departments," *IMF.* http://www.imf.org/external/np/pp/eng/2010/061510.pdf, (11/15/2013).

Montibeler, E. E. and E.S. Gallego. 2012. "Relaciones Bilaterales Entre Brasil y Liga Árabe: Un Análisis a Partir de la Teoría de la Internacionalización de la Producción y de la Diversificación Comercial." *Observatorio de la Economía Latinoamericana*, (163).

Mookerji, N. 2013. "Walmart Continues to Bide Its Time over Bharti Investment," *Business Standard.* http://www.business-standard.com/article/companies/walmart-continues-to-bide-its-time-over-bharti-investment-113081600670_1.html, (12/15/2013).

Moore, M. 2005. "Signposts to More Effective States: Responding to Governance Challenges in Developing Countries," *Institute of Developing Studies, The Centre for the Future State, UK,* http://www2.ids.ac.uk/gdr/cfs/pdfs/SignpoststoMoreEffectiveStates.pdf, (12/10/2013).

Mortished, C. 2008. "Russia Shows Its Political Clout by Hosting BRIC Summit". *The Times.* http://www.thetimes.co.uk/tto/business/markets/russia/article2143017.ece, (05/12/2012).

Mutum, D.P., S.K. Roy, and E. Kipnis (Eds.). 2014. *Marketing Cases from Emerging Markets.* New York, NY: Springer.

Nath, R. 2011. "Qaboos Fires 10 Ministers," *Khaleej Times*, Muscat, UAE. http://www.khaleejtimes.com/displayarticle.asp?xfile=data/middleeast/2011/March/middleeast_March140.xml&section=middleeast&col=, (10/12/2013).

Nilekani, N. 2008. *Imagining India: The Idea of a Renewed Nation.* New York City, NY: Penguin Group.

O'Neill, J. 2001. "Building Better Global Economic BRICs," *Global Economics Paper No. 66,* Goldman Sachs. http://www.goldmansachs.com/our-thinking/archive/archive-pdfs/build-better-brics.pdf, (12/17/2011).

O'Neill, J. 2005. "How Solid Are the BRICS," *Goldman Sachs' Global Economics Paper No. 134.* http://www.goldmansachs.com/our-thinking/archive/archive-pdfs/how-solid.pdf. (11.14.2012).

O'Neill, J. 2011. *The Growth Map: Economic Opportunity in the BRICs and Beyond.* Penguin Group, p. 125.

O'Sullivan, A.; M. E. Rey; and M. J. Galvez. 2011. "Opportunities and Challenges in the MENA Region." *The Arab world competitiveness report, 2011–2012, World Economic Forum.* http://www.weforum.org/reports/arab-world-competitiveness-report-2011-2012, (Last accessed on 01/02/2014).

OECD. 2007. Overview by the DAC Chair, In Development Co-operation Report. Vol. 8(1), chapter 1 (Paris, France: OECD, 2007).

Organization for Economic Co-operation and Development. 2013. "Economic Surveys and Country Surveillance: Economic Survey of Japan 2013," *OECD.* http://www.oecd.org/eco/surveys/economic-survey-japan.htm, (11/05/2013).

Organization for Economic Co-operation and Development. 2013. "Economic Surveys and Country Surveillance: Economic Survey of South Africa 2013," *OECD,* http://www.oecd.org/eco/surveys/economic-survey-south-africa.htm, (11/05/2103).

Orgaz, L.; L. Molina and C. Carrasco. 2011. "In El Creciente Peso de las Economias Emergentes en la Economia y Gobernanza Mundiales, Los Paises BRIC", *Documentos Ocasionales numero 1101*, Banco de Espana, Eurosistema. http://www.bde.es/f/webbde/SES/Secciones/Publicaciones/Publicaciones Seriadas/DocumentosOcasionales/11/Fich/do1101.pdf, (12/12/12).

Oxford Business Group's Staff Writers. 2013. "Brunei Darussalam Lpoks to Its Labs for Growth," *Brunei Darussalam,* http://www.oxfordbusinessgroup.com/economic_updates/brunei-darussalam-looks-its-labs-growth, (11/02/2013).

Pacek, N. and D. Thorniley. 2007. *Emerging Markets: Lessons for Business and the Outlook for Different markets (2nd edition).* London: The Economist and Profile Books.

Pain, N.; I. Koske; and M. Sollie. 2006. "Globalization and Inflation in the OECD Economies," *Economics Department Working Paper No. 524*, OECD, Paris. http://www.oecd.org/eco/42503918.pdf, (11/12/2013).

Papademos, L. 2006. "Globalization, Inflation, Imbalances and Monetary Policy," *Bank for International Settlement*, St. Louis, U.S., http://www.bis.org/review/r060607d.pdf, (11/09/2013).

Peterson, S. 2011. "Egypt's revolution redefines what's possible in the Arab world," *The Christian Science Monitor*, http://www.csmonitor.com/layout/set/r14/World/Middle-East/2011/0211/Egypt-s-revolution-redefines-what-s-possible-in-the-Arab-world, (11/10/2013).

Pettis, M. 2013. *The Great Rebalancing: Trade, Conflict, and the Perilous Road Ahead for the World Economy*, Princeton University Press.

Pigato, M. 2009. *Strengthening China's and India's Trade and Investment Ties to the Middle East and North Africa.* Washington DC: The World Bank.

Portes, R. 2010. *Currency Wars and the Emerging-Market Countries*. *VoxEU*, http://www.voxeu.org/article/currency-wars-and-emerging-markets.

Posadas, A. 2000. "Combating Corruption Under International Law," *Duke University Journal of Comparative and International Law*, pages 345-414, http://scholarship.law.duke.edu/djcil/vol10/iss2/4, (12/02/2013).

Qatar National Bank (QNB Group). 2013."US, Eurozone Deflation Calls for 'Expansionary policy'." http://www.qnb.com.qa/cs/Satellite?c=QNBNews_C&cid=1355402782038&locale=|1344242931312&p=1344242934398&pagename=QNBSingapore percent2FQNBLayout

Qiang, H. 2013. "ASEAN Businesses See Integration as Opportunity, Not Threat: Survey," *The English News*, Xinhua, China, http://news.xinhuanet.com/english/business/2013-12/11/c_132960344.htm, (12/11/2013).

Radu, P. C. 2008. "The Investigative Journalist Handbook," *International Center for Journalist*, https://reportingproject.net/occrp/index.php/en/cc-resource-center/handbook/191-the-investigative-journalist-handbook, (09/08/2012).

Rai, V. and W. Simon. 2008. *Think India*. New York, NY.: Penguin Group.

Rashid, A. (2012). *Pakistan on the Brink: The Future of America, Pakistan, and Afghanistan*. New York, NY: Viking/Penguin Group.

Reinhart, C. M. and M. B. Sbrancia. 2011. "The Liquidation of Government Debt", *NBER Working Paper 16893*. http://www.nber.org/papers/w16893, (03/02/12).

Reinhart, C.M. and J.F. Kirkegaard. 2012. "Financial Repression: Then and Now," *Vox*, http://www.voxeu.org/article/financial-repression-then-and-now, (04/23/12).

Rich, B.R. and L. Janos. 1994. *Skunk Works: A Personal Memoir of My Years at Lockheed*. New York: Little Brown & Co., 1994, p. 10.

Richter, F. 2011. "Protester killed in Bahrain 'Day of Rage'," *Reuters*, http://uk.reuters.com/article/2011/02/14/uk-bahrain-protests-idUKTRE71D1G520110214, (11/02/2013).

Rickards, J. 2011. *Currency Wars: The Making of the Next Global Crisis*, Penguin/Portfolio Group.

Rodrik, D. 2009. *Growth after the Crisis*. Cambridge, MA.: Harvard Kennedy School

Roudi, F. 2001. "Population Trends and Challenges in the MENA," *PRB*. http://www.prb.org/Publications/Reports/2001/PopulationTrendsandChallengesintheMiddleEastandNorthAfrica.aspx, (12/20/2013).

RT Staff Writers. 2013. "BRICS Agree to Capitalize Development Bank at $100bn," *RT*, http://rt.com/business/russia-brics-bank-g20-468/, (last accessed on 11/06/2013).

Sallum, M.N. 2013. "Potencial a explorar é enorme." *Agência de Notícias Brasil-Árabe.* http://www.anba.com.br/, (01/03/2014).

Schmidt, V. 2003. "French Capitalism Transformed; Yet Still a Third Variety of Capitalism." *Economy and Society,* 32(4). http://www.vedegylet.hu/fejkrit/szvggyujt/schmidt_frenchCapitalism.pdf

Schwab, Klaus. 2013. "The Global Competitiveness Report 2012-2013," *World Economic Forum,* http://www3.weforum.org/docs/WEF_GlobalCompetitivenessReport_2012-13.pdf, (Last accessed on 08/12/2013).

Schwartz, N. 2013. "Growth Gain Blurs Signs of Weakness in Economy," *New York Times,* http://www.nytimes.com/2013/11/08/business/economy/us-economy-grows-at-2-8-rate-in-third-quarter.html?_r=0, (11/10/2013).

Senkovich, V. 2013. "The Arab World's Potential Importance to Russia's Economy." *Russian International Affairs Council.* http://russiancouncil.ru/en/inner/?id_4=1548#top, (01/03/2014).

Seyid, S. O. 2011. "Mauritania Police Crush Protest - Doctors Announce Strike," *Radio Netherlands Worldwide,* Africa Desk, Mauritania. http://www.rnw.nl/africa/article/mauritania-police-crush-protest-doctors-announce-strike, (12/12/2012).

Shahminan, F. 2013. "Brunei Economy to Grow 2.4pc in Next Four Years," *Dawn.com,* http://www.dawn.com/news/1048280/brunei-economy-to-grow-24pc-in-next-four-years, (10/10/2013).

Smith & Nephew Corporate. 2012. "Smith & Nephew Reaches Settlement with US Government," *Smith & Nephew,* http://www.smith-nephew.com/news-and-media/news/smith-and-nephew-reaches-settlement-with-us-gover/, (12/12/2013).

Snyder, M. 2012. "45 Signs That China Is Colonizing America," *End of The American Dream,* http://endoftheamericandream.com/archives/45-signs-that-china-is-colonizing-america, (09/08/2013).

Soubbotina, T.P. and K.A. Sheram. 2004. *Beyond Economic Growth: An Introduction to Sustainable Development,* World Bank, 2nd edition.

Spencer, R. 2011. "Libya: Civil War Breaks Out as Gaddafi Mounts Rearguard Fight," *The Telegraph,* http://www.telegraph.co.uk/news/worldnews/africaandindianocean/libya/8344034/Libya-civil-war-breaks-out-as-Gaddafi-mounts-rearguard-fight.html, (11/12/2013).

Stern, M. 2012. "International Trade: CIVETS Economies," *Financial Director Newspaper,* London, UK. http://www.financialdirector.co.uk/financial-director/feature/2169190/international-trade-civets-economies, (11/03/2013).

Svensson, L. E. O. 2008. "Inflation Targeting," in S. N. Durlauf and L. E. Blume (Eds.), *The New Palgrave Dictionary of Economics, 2nd edition.* Palgrave Macmillan.

Taborda, J. 2013. "Death of the Dollar 2014: Euro Area GDP Growth Rate," *Trading Economics*, http://www.tradingeconomics.com/euro-area/gdp-growth, (12/15/2013).

Khanna, T. and K.G. Palepu. 2010. *Winning in Emerging Markets: A Roadmap for Strategy and Execution*. Boston: Harvard Business School Publishing.

Telegraph Staff Writers. 2013. "Next Chief Lord Wolfson Launches £250,000 Prize to Solve Housing Crisis." *The Telegraph*, http://www.telegraph.co.uk/finance/newsbysector/constructionandproperty/10448303/Next-chief-Lord-Wolfson-launches-250000-prize-to-solve-housing-crisis.html, (12/11/2013).

The FCPA Blog. 2012, "Biomet Pays $22.8 Million To Settle Bribe Charges," *The FCPA Blog*, http://www.fcpablog.com/blog/2012/3/26/biomet-pays-228-million-to-settle-bribe-charges.html#, (09/09/2012).

Transparency International Secretariat. 2013. "Media Advisory: Major Exporters Still Lag in Enforcing Rules Against Foreign Bribery," *Transparency International*, http://www.transparency.org/news/pressrelease/bribe_paying_still_very_high_worldwide_but_people_ready_to_fight_back, (12/14/2013).

U.S. Department of Justice. 2012. "Marubeni Corporation Resolves Foreign Corrupt Practices Act Investigation and Agrees to Pay a $54.6 Million Criminal Penalty," *U.S. Department of Justice*, http://www.justice.gov/opa/pr/2012/January/12-crm-060.html, (07/02/2013).

Vaidya, S. 2011. "One Dead, Dozens Injured as Oman Protest Turns Ugly," *Gulf News*, Oman, http://gulfnews.com/news/gulf/oman/one-dead-dozen-injured-as-oman-protest-turns-ugly-1.768789, (11/01/2013).

Vale Columbia Center on Sustainable International Investment. 2009. "First Ranking Survey of Mexican Multinationals Finds Grey Diversity of Industries," *Columbia Law School*, http://www.vcc.columbia.edu/files/vale/documents/EMGP-Mexico-Report-Final-09Dec09.pdf, (11/30/2013).

Wagstyl, S. 2013. "Eurasia: Emerging Markets Are World's 'Top Risk' for 2013," *Financial Times*, http://blogs.ft.com/beyond-brics/2013/01/07/eurasia-emerging-markets-are-worlds-top-risk-for-2013/#axzz2nkpeGUB7, (12/17/2013).

Weggel, O. 2006. "Cambodia in 2005: Year of Reassurance". *Asian Survey* 46 (1): 158.

Welch, D. and T. Weidlich. 2012. "Wal-Mart Bribery Probe May Exposes Retailer to U.S. Fines," *Bloomberg*, http://www.bloomberg.com/news/2012-04-23/wal-mart-bribery-probe-may-exposes-retailer-to-u-s-fines.html, (04/23/2012).

Werr, P. 2013. "Egypt's Economy to Miss Government Growth Forecasts: Reuters Poll," *Reuters* Cairo, Egypt, http://www.reuters.com/article/2013/10/01/us-economy-egypt-poll-idUSBRE99012O20131001., (10/30/2013).

Wheatley, A. 2013. "Emerging markets thrive as eurozone suffers," *The International News,* http://www.thenews.com.pk/Todays-News-3-167386-Emerging-markets-thrive-as-eurozone-suffers, (Last accessed on 11/10/2013).

Williams, R. 1983. *Capitalism (Revised Edition).* Oxford: Oxford University Press.

Wilson, D. and R. Purushothaman. 2003. "Dreaming with BRICs: The Path to 2050," *Global Economics Paper No. 99,* Goldman Sachs,, http://www.goldmansachs.com/our-thinking/archive/archive-pdfs/brics-dream.pdf, (04/05/11).

World Bank Staff Writers. 2012. "World Development Indicators Database. Gross Domestic Product 2011," *The World Bank,* http://data.worldbank.org/data-catalog/world-development-indicators, (09/22/2012).

World Bank Staff Writers. 2013. "Doing Business: Measuring Business Regulations," *The World Bank,* http://www.doingbusiness.org/rankings, (09/22/2012).

World Bank Staff Writers. 2013. "An Update on Vietnam's Recent Economic Development July 2013: Key Findings," *The World Bank,* http://www.worldbank.org/en/news/feature/2013/07/12/taking-stock-july-2013-an-update-on-vietnams-recent-economic-development-key-findings, (11/05/2013).

World Bank Staff Writers. 2013. "Doing Business: Ease of Doing Business in Colombia," *The World Bank,* http://www.doingbusiness.org/data/exploreeconomies/colombia/, (06/12/2013).

World Bank Staff Writers. 2013. "Tourism in the Arab World Can Mean More Than Sun, Sand and Beaches," *The World Bank,* http://www.worldbank.org/en/news/feature/2013/02/11/tourism-in-the-arab-world-can-mean-more-than-sun-sand-and-beaches, (01/03/2014).

World Bank. 2008. *Middle East and North Africa Region 2007 Economic Developments and Prospects : Job Creation in an Era of High Growth.* Washington, DC: World Bank. http://documents.worldbank.org/curated/en/2008/06/9520526/middle-east-north-africa-region-2007-economic-developments-prospects-job-creation-era-high-growth.

Young, V. 2006. "Macquarie launches Australia's first BRIC funds," *InvestorDaily,* http://www.investordaily.com.au/25542-macquarie-launches-australias-first-bric-funds, (05/23/2007).

Zoffer, J. 2012. "Future of Dollar Hegemony," *The Harvard International Review,* http://hir.harvard.edu/crafting-the-city/future-of-dollar-hegemony, (10/12/2012).

Index

OTHER TITLES FROM THE ECONOMICS COLLECTION

Philip Romero, The University of Oregon and Jeffrey Edwards,
North Carolina A&T State University, Editors

- *Innovative Pricing Strategies to Increase Profits* by Daniel Marburger
- *Regression for Economics* by Shahdad Naghshpour
- *Statistics for Economics* by Shahdad Naghshpour
- *How Strong Is Your Firm's Competitive Advantage?* by Daniel Marburger
- *A Primer on Microeconomics* by Thomas Beveridge
- *Game Theory: Anticipating Reactions for Winning Actions* by Mark L. Burkey
- *A Primer on Macroeconomics* by Thomas Beveridge
- *Economic Decision Making Using Cost Data: A Guide for Managers* by Daniel Marburger
- *The Fundamentals of Money and Financial Systems* by Shahdad Naghshpour
- *International Economics: Understanding the Forces of Globalization for Managers* by Paul Torelli
- *The Economics of Crime* by Zagros Madjd-Sadjadi
- *Money and Banking: An Intermediate Market-Based Approach* by William D. Gerdes
- *Basel III Liquidity Regulation and Its Implications* by Mark A. Petersen and Janine Mukuddem-Petersen
- *Saving American Manufacturing: The Fight for Jobs, Opportunity, and National Security* by William R. Killingsworth
- *What Hedge Funds Really Do: An Introduction to Portfolio Management* by Philip J. Romero and Tucker Balch
- *Advanced Economies and Emerging Markets: Prospects for Globalization* by Marcus Goncalves, José Alves, Carlos Frota, Harry Xia, and Rajabahadur V. Arcot

Announcing the Business Expert Press Digital Library

*Concise E-books Business Students Need
for Classroom and Research*

This book can also be purchased in an e-book collection by your library as
- a one-time purchase,
- that is owned forever,
- allows for simultaneous readers,
- has no restrictions on printing, and
- can be downloaded as PDFs from within the library community.

Our digital library collections are a great solution to beat the rising cost of textbooks. E-books can be loaded into their course management systems or onto students' e-book readers.

The **Business Expert Press** digital libraries are very affordable, with no obligation to buy in future years. For more information, please visit **www.businessexpertpress.com/librarians**. To set up a trial in the United States, please email **sales@businessexpertpress.com**.

www.ingramcontent.com/pod-product-compliance
Lightning Source LLC
Chambersburg PA
CBHW060558210326
41519CB00014B/3512